INNOCENCE AND SPICE

True Short Stories with the Warm, Humorous Utterances of Children

Bob Cushman

Copyright © 2018 Bob Cushman

All rights reserved.

ISBN:0692187561
ISBN-13: 978-0692187562 (Cushman Books)

To my own wonderful kids: Marilyn, Bob Jr., and Charlotte, who, though now adults, did, in their childhood, come forth with some of the gems appearing in the final pages of this book. And to Ramona (Romie) Cushman, this world's most wonderful daughter-in-law, who created the illustrations for this book. And to Chuck George and Dan Van Bogart, my sons-in-law, just so they won't feel left out!

CONTENTS

Foreword by Charlotte Cushman

Acknowledgements

Preface

1	Come Read Our Stories	Page 1
2	The Author Remembers His Own Childhood	Page 244
3	A Few Stories of the Author's Kids	Page 251
4	A Kid of the Author Remembers More Stories	Page 263

FOREWORD

My father loved children. He loved their innocence and the straightforward way they deal with the world. When they would make a remark that tickled him, he would laugh and then rush to his desk to write it down so that the tale would not be forgotten. When exactly he came up with the idea of writing this book, I don't remember, but he took great pride in it and his one last wish was that we, his kids, would see to it that it was published; because, unfortunately, he died before he could see it come to fruition.

Dad died in 1994. It seems so long ago, and at the same time, just like yesterday.

Dad, your kids have had their own kids. Those kids have grown up and are now having their own kids. We set aside your wish because of all those kids. Children, one of the greatest joys in life, took up a lot of our time, but they were worth every second, every minute, every hour. You instilled that in us by how you raised us, listened to us and taught us. And, most importantly, how you loved us.

So now, here it is twenty-four years later and we finally got it done. Thanks, Dad, for all you gave us. And thanks for helping us to appreciate and enjoy the innocence and spice of the mind of the child.

Charlotte Cushman

ACKNOWLEDGEMENTS

A huge thank you to everyone who gave my dad laughter and joy by sharing the stories of their children.

Thank you to Romie Cushman for the illustrations. I know that Dad liked and appreciated them.

Thank you to Kay Hall who typed most of this book into the computer. Dad had done it on a typewriter before computers became commonly used.

Thanks to those who gave feedback, gave suggestions and spent time editing this book: Dan Van Bogart, Charles George and Jacqueline Lehman. Thanks to Melissa DeLong for helping with the cover.

And thank you to all the children who provided and continue to provide us with their innocence and spice.

PREFACE

Whoever first said, "Truth is stranger than fiction," must have been thinking of the utterances of children, for who in his most imaginative moment could think up the gems that tumble forth from the mouths of babes? Here, indeed, is a source of warmth and humor with which even the agile mind of the most creative writer would be hard pressed to compete.

It cannot be inferred that this is because a writer's thoughts are confined to more logical avenues. Very often, upon careful examination, a child's conclusion regarding a given situation is found to be extremely logical, given, of course, the child's context.

We are told that children learn to use computers more readily than adults because they have not fallen into the mental ruts that ensnare our imaginations as we grow older. Thus, too, this same agility of the young mind, unshackled by habit and the implied and explicit pressures to conform, is what provides us with the jewels of innocence and spice that never cease to charm us.

In gathering material for this book, I have solicited in various ways only true stories about small children, most of which conclude with the warm, humorous, unexpected utterance of the child. I have made every effort to avoid anything that has been in print previously.

I was tempted by a story, the source of which I could not pinpoint, but I suspected it might have gone the rounds as a 'joke' and probably had appeared in print. This was about the small boy who burst out crying when the friendly, lumbering St. Bernard walked up and started licking him. The boy's mother tried to quiet and reassure the boy, but he screamed and declared that the animal was going to eat him up. His mother told him that the dog was just being friendly and had no thought of eating him, whereupon the boy asked, "Well, then why was he tasting me?"

A gentleman who had seen my solicitation for stories on a super market bulletin board phoned me and requested that I tell him more specifically the type of thing I wanted. I emphasized my desire for true, uncirculated stories involving the cute and unexpected responses of small children to situations or conversations. I then proceeded to give him a couple of examples of the material I was using. In the second example, I told him of the mother who was preparing to take her son to the doctor. The lad had new shoes; she was running late when she noticed the child had his shoes on the wrong feet and ordered, "You get those shoes off and get them on the other feet and be quick about it." At this point, my caller interrupted and said, "And the kid says, 'I don't have any other feet.' Oh, that's an old one. That's been around for years!" To say I was chagrined would be the understatement of the decade! You may be sure the story was forthwith deleted from my stockpile!

Of course, it cannot be ruled out that more than one mother might have had that very experience. Nevertheless, if I have had any clue that a story has "been the rounds," it will not be found in these pages.

But even with this said, I ask you not to judge me harshly if you find here a story similar to one you have heard. After all, there are millions of kids sounding off daily, and the similarities of situations to which they react are bound to produce duplication.

For example, my stories "Financial Center" and "Oriental Cuisine" (all stories in this book appear alphabetically according to title except those in the final pages which are stories from my own experience) are, due to the nature of the situations they encompass, stories that surely must, sometime, somewhere, in essence have been duplicated. However, inasmuch as these came to me from sources whose reliability I do not question, I have no qualms in including them.

One further word: In many of these stories, the child's age may not be crucial to the amusement factor. However, in others, the reader must consider the child's tender age in order to savor the impact of his or her utterance. Thus it is with my story about Julie when she was only three. The probability that she knew anything whatsoever about Eros seemed strictly nil, and yet, well, you'll see when you read "Not So Secret Weapon."

So, now…

Come read our Stories

ACCENT ON EXPERIENCE

At the family reunion, five-year-old Kellie was to bunk in the same room with her nine-year-old cousin, Jennifer.

Jennifer was ready to sack out, but Kellie was put to bed under protest. In fact, the latter refused to settle down, used all the old excuses for getting up and joining the adults and even invented new ones apropos to family reunions, such as, "But this is the first time I've even met Uncle Roger, and he's leaving early in the morning."

Each time Kellie was ushered back to the bedroom, Jennifer was roused and she wasn't happy about having her slumber interrupted.

Finally, when Kellie got up again, Jennifer followed her out to the living room, sputtering about being unable to sleep because of "that brat!"

Kellie's mother took her firmly by the arm, gave her a good swat on the behind and roughly led her back to the bedroom with, of course, an appropriate warning. The child began to cry.

With the door closed, the sobbing could be heard in the living room. After a few minutes of this, it became evident that Grandma could not stand it much longer. An unmistakable expression of sympathy was showing in her eyes. She rose and took three steps toward the bedroom.

"Don't do it, Grandma, don't do it," said Jennifer. "She's just trying to make you feel sorry for her so she'll get her own way. I know. I do it all the time!"

ACUTE NEED

It is common practice for a child to pick up something that catches his eye near the checkout counter and then try to persuade his parent to buy it.

Thus it seemed like a routine event when seven-year-old Mike picked up a package of Certs as his father approached the cashier's post of the fancy restaurant after having treated three generations to Mother's Day dinner.

"Daddy, can we buy these?"

"No, put them back."

"But Daddy, please."

"I said 'no!'"

"Please, Daddy?"

Now it is a well-known strategy, universally used, very often successful, wherein the child raises his voice with each pleading. In the presence of guests or strangers, this is one of the purer forms of intimidation.

In this case, the crescendo increased; other patrons stopped their conversations and turned to listen, as father fairly shouted, "No, I said 'n, o, no' and that's final!"

This climax having been reached, complete silence ensued, and then came the final, persuasive argument:

"But Daddy, we need them. Grandma has bad breath!"

ADJUSTING TO THE TIMES

Tommy had flown in airplanes, and, as a matter of fact, his Uncle Fred was a commercial airline pilot, but this was no big deal.

No big deal, that is, until one day his uncle took him into the cockpit of a Boeing 747. The child was awe-struck when he saw the lights and dials, the push buttons and levers, on all sides and even overhead. Spellbound, he didn't say much as he gazed in wide-eyed wonderment. There was an occasional question, an occasional "oh."

This all changed however by the next time he saw his uncle. "Uncle Fred," he said, "I've decided when I grow up I'm going to be an airline pilot like you. Would you teach me, Uncle Fred? Would you?"

His uncle chuckled and ruffled the boy's hair, "Tommy, probably by the time you grow up, airline pilots will be obsolete."

"Oh, well, that's all right. Then you teach me to be an ob-sleet pilot, I learn real easy!"

ADVANCED CULINARY PROCEDURES

Heidi, Julie and Benny were staying with Grandma. Some kind of commotion was going on in the basement, the sound of frequent flushing of the stool and lots of jabbering and squealing.

Thinking it was time to investigate, Grandma descended the stairway to find three heads leaning over the toilet stool, a river of water on the floor, running over toward the drain and four-year-old Benny actively pumping the flush lever.

Research disclosed that in the stool were unnumbered fragments of a Coca-Cola bottle and three raw potatoes. What a mess!

Grandma ordered the children to take off their shoes and stockings and get upstairs. Then she began the arduous clean up. With the flush lever released, the water ceased flowing, and the river receded. Gradually the excess water in the bowl seeped on down past the obstructions, leveling off at the normal depth. Gingerly Grandma reached in and removed the larger pieces of the bottle. The potatoes were embedded with glass slivers so she could not grasp them firmly, and they were stuck tight.

She tried using a screwdriver to dislodge the potatoes, but she only chipped off some small pieces. Upstairs she went and put a kettle of water on to boil, then it was back to bail the excess water out of the stool. The kettle began to whistle, so up the stairs she went again.

"What are you doing, Grandma?" Benny asked.

"Oh, you kids really know how to make a mess. I guess the only way I can get those potatoes out of that stool is to cook them to mush so they'll flush down. Tell me, just what on earth possessed you kids to do such a silly thing?" Of course there was no reply.

Down she went with the boiling water. Then up for another boiling pot, then down again. Up, down, up, down!

She heard the phone ring, but it rang only once, meaning one of the children had answered.

"Who is it?" she asked, after dashing back upstairs.

"It was Mom," Benny answered.

"What did she want?"

"She wanted to know if everything was all right."

"What did you tell her?"

"I said, 'Sure.'"

"Was that all?"

"She wanted to talk to you."

"Well, heavens' sakes, why didn't you call me?"

"I told her you couldn't come right now 'cause you were down in the basement cooking potatoes in the toilet!"

AH, VACATION!

Roger and Sue had been married for six years and now had Debbie, five, and Diana, three, to show for it. They had never taken a vacation—weekend trips, yes, but never a real vacation.

Now they were planning two weeks back in their Colorado homeland, and the term "vacation" was coming into frequent use around the house. Debbie understood, but "vacation" was only a word to Diana, and even though she told her playmates that they were going "on 'cation," she really did not understand the concept.

The budget demanded savings wherever possible, and the plan was to leave Friday evening, drive straight through from Hartford to Denver, a distance of two thousand miles, Roger and Sue alternately driving and sleeping, stopping only for restrooms, food and fuel. Needless to say, such an exercise can test family harmony. The children napped frequently but the strain nevertheless took its toll and the bickering escalated slowly but steadily.

After a fitful night's sleep everyone awoke at dawn on the third day. Almost immediately the bickering resumed between the children, and soon there was hitting and then crying. Roger, driving, yelled at the girls to desist, but the effect was only momentary. Finally he pulled over onto the shoulder, stopped and put on the brake. Then he turned around in his seat, grabbed Debbie, gave her a good swat on the bottom, then did the same with Diana. "Now I want this foolishness stopped and stopped now!" he commanded.

Both girls cried as though they had been flogged but quit fighting and sat tight in opposite corners of the back seat. The crying eventually subsided. Debbie dozed off. Diana sat motionless and quiet except for the catching of breath that follows sobbing.

Finally Diana spoke.

"Daddy?"

"Yes, Sweetie."

"Can I ask a question?"

"Of course, Sweetie, you may always ask a question. What is it?"

"Are we on 'cation yet?"

ALMOST, BUT NOT QUITE

Last year at the Kiwanis picnic, Joann had entered the fifty-yard foot race for the four-year-olds and had finished in second place. When Dad announced the date of this summer's picnic, the child began talking about the race and practicing for it.

Now she was at the starting line with the other five-year-olds. The gun sounded, and they were off. Immediately Joann was in the lead, running as fast as her legs would carry her. Spectators at the end of the track cheered and waved. Joann knew her parents were there pulling for her, but she felt her strength ebbing.

When she suddenly noticed that another girl had inched up and pulled ahead of her, she panicked, then put forth one final effort and spurted ahead, touching the wire just a split second before her competitor.

A cheer rose up from the crowd. Joann kept right on running to her parents and buried her head in her mother's skirt, crying.

Surprised and perplexed, her mother put her arms around the child saying, "Hey, come on, you little goose, what's wrong? You did beautifully, just beautifully."

Sobbing, the child responded, "Yes, I—I—I know, b—b—but I almost didn't win!"

AMAZING SKIN CONDITION

Usually Mom bathed three-year-old Amanda, but Mom was fighting the flu, and Dad was performing the chore this time.

"Don't get it too hot," Mom called from her bed when she heard the water running. "Amanda has very sensitive skin."

"Feel the water, Amanda," Dad said. "See if that's about right."

Amanda put her hand in the tub and stirred the water a bit. "No, Daddy, that's too hot," she said.

Dad turned off the hot faucet, letting the cold one continue to run. In a few seconds he said, "Okay, now try that."

Again the child put her hand in and stirred. "No, Daddy, that's still too hot, don't forget what Mama said. I have very sensible skin!"

A MOTHER'S REPRIEVE

It was in the sixties that Susan took her two daughters, Debbie, five, and Diana, three, to see the movie, *Hawaii*.

Early in the picture some of the historical background was given in spoken form, and the story was told of the voyage of some of the early settlers who came by canoe. Traveling from Bora Bora they had lost their way to Nuku Hiva and were distraught and frightened. Mano, a shark, had long been the personal god of Teura, one of the old women aboard the canoe, and this blue beast suddenly appeared in the waters near the canoe and told Teura, "There will be stars tonight, all the stars that you require to guide you,"—indeed a stirring legend.

Later on in the movie, an explicit incident of childbirth is shown, rather extended and with the mother crying out in agony during the ordeal.

Very shortly after the childbirth scene there was an intermission.

"Mommy," Debbie said, "I have a question about the movie."

Now only a scant quarter of a century ago, childbirth was not as openly talked about as it is today. Add to that, at that time, Susan was more or less the timid sort, and add also that she had put off explaining to the children, at their tender ages, even where babies came from.

"Oh heavens," she thought to herself. "Here it comes. How am I going to handle this? This is neither the time nor the place." (As though there ever would be a time and place!)

She braced herself. "Okay Debbie," she said, "What is your question?"

"Mommy, what was the name of that shark again?"

AMPUTATION MAYBE, BUT NOT THIS

Tender ears often pick up words and even concepts not really intended for them. Leslie lived in a normal cable TV home where, when videos were discussed, there was sometimes mention of "dirty" shows, with the implication that they had "naughty" aspects. The usual discussions and terms were occasionally part of the conversation in which Leslie did not participate but to which her ears were well attuned.

One day her mother fell and injured her ankle. She limped around the rest of the day, but the pain grew worse and she had a fitful night. The next morning Dad took a day off work in order to take her to the doctor for an examination of the injured limb.

The next-door neighbor came in to sit with Leslie and after about an hour, Dad phoned back to give the sitter an estimate of the time they would probably return home. The sitter relayed the information to Leslie, and in their conversation the child was told of the probable test that her mother would undergo. Leslie looked confused. Slowly the corners of her mouth turned down, her lip quivered, and she began to cry.

"Honey," the sitter said, "it's going to be all right. They'll be able to make your mommy comfortable. They'll do whatever they need to, and she's going to be all right."

But the child was little consoled and blurted out, "But I don't want my mommy to be X-rated!"

ANSWER THAT ONE, DAD

Brian's and Kevin's weekly allowance was specifically tied to the performance of certain chores that they were expected to perform routinely.

As with most children, there were occasional lapses, which resulted in the allowance being withheld or reduced. The sticks that had fallen from the trees in Wednesday's storm were still on the lawn when allowance time rolled around on Saturday. Kevin collected his allowance in full, but to Brian, Dad said, "Sorry Son, you've had three days to pick up the sticks, but you preferred to goof off—no allowance this week."

Then he launched forth into a further lecture: "Son," he said, "you've got to learn that you don't get anything in this world without earning it. Life isn't easy. It takes work to get something of value. Everything that's worth anything must be earned. It just doesn't come automatically."

"Oh, you just don't love me. Kevin always gets his allowance. You never did love me, you never did."

"Brian, that's silly. It's because I do love you that I want to teach you. If I teach you while you're young, it'll be easier for you when you're grown up; you won't be expecting to get something for nothing. Of course, I love you. I've loved you since the day you were born."

"You loved me when I was born?" Brian asked.

"Yes, of course I did, you had my love from the very minute you were born."

"Oh? How come I had your love when I was born? I hadn't earned it!"

ANYHOW, GRANDPA STARTED IT

When Grandpa came to visit, eleven-year-old Missy, gave up her bed and moved in with eight-year-old Charly where she slept on a mattress on the floor. All went well for five days. Then the children got in a row; how it started, nobody knew, and it didn't matter, but they were determined to end the sleeping arrangements.

"I hate that dumb Missy," Charly declared, "I want her out of my room. She has to have that dumb light on all night and I can't sleep."

"That Charly's impossible," Missy countered, "and besides he plays that darn radio and who can sleep with that dumb thing on!"

They ranted on, and the argument escalated until finally Mother said, "Okay, now, I've heard enough. Missy, tonight you'll bring your mattress and sleep in our room; I'll not hear another word about it. Case closed!"

Dinner over. Dishes done. Bedtime.

"Okay Missy, bring your mattress to our room and get ready for bed."

But by this time the breach had been mended, forgotten.

"Oh, gee, Mom, I want to sleep in Charly's room."

"Oh, no, he's impossible, remember, and you can't stand his radio."

"Yeah Mom, it's all right," Charly chimed in. "We want to sleep together."

"Oh no, you hate your sister, and you can't sleep with her dumb light on."

"Oh, come on, Mom," Charly protested, "you know me. That was just me and my big mouth!"

AREN'T THEY ALL?

Dawn had been the flower girl at her older sister's wedding and was explaining the ceremony to one of her little friends.

"I don't really remember all the big words," she said, "but it starts off with the minister saying, 'Dearly beloved, we are gathered here with God to join this man and this woman in holy…something,' and then he says some more stuff, and then he said to my sister, 'Do you take this man to be your awfully wedded husband?'"

A SPRING MATTRESS MIGHT DO

Freddie waited impatiently in line to be able to visit with Santa. At long last he was sitting there, next to the round little belly and looking up into the kindly, bewhiskered face.

After the usual introductory patter, Santa asked, "What would you like me to bring you for Christmas?"

"A waterbed."

"A waterbed? Do your mommy and daddy have a waterbed?"

"No."

"Did you ever sleep on a waterbed?"

"No."

"Well, if you've never slept on one, what makes you think you'd like to have a waterbed?"

"Because sometimes at night I get thirsty!"

AUXILIARY HEATER

Why they had to go shopping this particular Saturday morning, Connie couldn't understand. After the frost was scraped from the window, it was plainly seen that the thermometer stood at six degrees below zero. Connie could see Dad out there brushing the snow from the windshield and rear window, trying to hold his hat on and shield his face from the stinging wind.

Dad had started the engine, and white steam was pouring from the exhaust pipe, then pummeled into immediate dissipation by the swirling breeze. Dad got in the car and tooted the horn.

"Come on," Connie called to her mother and older brother, Dan, "Daddy's ready." She trudged out to the car, got in the back seat and sat down. She shivered and her teeth chattered. "Turn on the heat, Daddy, I'm freezing," she said.

"I've got it on, Honey, but it'll take a few minutes for it to heat up."

Dad tooted the horn again and finally the others came. Mom got in the front and Dan opened the door next to Connie. "Scoot over, Connie," he said.

"Nuts to you," came Connie's quick reply. "You go around; I've warmed up one seat. I'm not gonna warm up a second one!"

BABY FROM THE MELON PATCH?

Cynthia, age three, had been next door playing with her friend, Carla. The latter had a baby brother, only eleven days old, and Cynthia had been allowed to look at the baby and even touch his soft skin.

All this Cynthia reported to her parents, and then…pensively, "Mommy, where do babies come from?"

"Don't lie to her, don't lie to her," her husband whispered grinning.

"Well," Cynthia's mother replied, "after two people get married, God plants a seed in the mother's tummy. The seed is nourished by the mother's body until it develops into a full-grown baby, just like Carla's new little brother, and then it is delivered from the mommy's body."

Her parents were a bit surprised that the child accepted the explanation routinely—no further questions—no big deal.

A few days later, Dad brought home a watermelon. At dessert time, Cynthia dove into a large slice and was enjoying it with great gusto. Abruptly, she stopped chewing, then spit out a glob of the melon. From this she separated out a seed with her fork, then carefully picked out all seeds remaining in the slice—even the little undeveloped ones—and poked them to the edge of her plate.

"Oh, boy," she said, "I don't want to swallow any of these, I don't want a baby growing inside my tummy!"

BAD BREAK, DUE TO BREAK IN BRAKE

Nine-year-old Mark was furious. His bike had a flat tire, and when his older brother, Bill, and their friend Kevin, decided to take off on a bike ride, Mark had pleaded with them to fix his flat so that he could accompany them. But although the trio usually functioned as a friendly team, disdain prevailed this time as the older boys found no time to help the "youngster."

Bill and Kevin took off, leaving Mark fuming. Bill's brake was not working properly, so when the boys returned home, Bill and Kevin removed the brake and took it into the basement for repair. Just as they were returning to replace it on the bike, Mark, his bike still disabled, jumped on Bill's bike for revenge and took off, peddling furiously down a long hill.

Bill and Kevin, aware that the younger boy was seriously endangered because he did not know that he had no brake, ran after him, yelling out the warning. Mark simply assumed they were chasing him because he had riled them by "stealing" Bill's bike.

Down the hill they raced—Mark, on wheels peddling as fast as he could move his legs, outpaced the runners. Bill and Kevin were terrified, knowing the lad was headed for a heavily trafficked cross street at the bottom of the hill with no way to curtail his speed.

Suddenly Mark was there. He applied what he thought was the brake. No response whatsoever. He continued, speeding into what now seemed certain disaster. In a panic he turned at a sharp angle, banking to the point that the bike was almost horizontal. Now, devoid of traction, the bike slid sideways toward the traffic.

Mark gave a mighty push to free himself from the bike, and then thrust himself into a roll toward the curb. He was severely bumped and bruised, but alive. Not so the bike; it met its demise under the wheels of a semi-trailer truck.

Such are the vicissitudes of childhood trios!

BANE OF INTERSTELLAR TRAVEL

Mike knew it all. Well, why shouldn't he? After all, at five years of age, he was a whole year older than his cousin, Craig. Craig, in Mike's eyes, was just a youngster. In any conversation the pair had, the elder Mike felt obligated to inform the child, Craig, of the true facts of the situation.

It was in the early days of the space program and Mike was telling Craig all about it.

"They shoot 'em up into the air just like sky rockets."

"Where do they do it?"

"They shoot 'em up from Cape Kennedy down in Florida. It's named after President Kennedy."

"Gee, you mean they have people on 'em, those rockets?"

"No, not now, but in a few years, they're going to send people up in 'em."

"Well, gee, where do they go?" Craig asked.

This rather stumped Mike. He had been so awed by the fact that the huge missiles actually hurled into the air, and then far out into space, that he hadn't paused to consider where they were going.

He had to think fast. After all, he couldn't have the younger lad thinking he didn't have the answers. "Why…why, they go up there in the sky and land on the stars, of course."

"Oh gee, that's crazy. They couldn't do that," Craig countered.

"Why not?" Mike asked as though he feared he had made a statement which could be proved wrong.

"Cause, they couldn't land on the stars with all those points sticking out!"

BEANS

Innocence allows some latitude where an utterance might otherwise be viewed askance.

It was a perfectly normal bodily function, but evidently it was a first for three-year-old Rosalie, or at least the first time noticed.

What she had eaten was not reported; the way she expressed it was, "Oops, I burped on my bottom!"

BEDTIME STORY

In preparation for their vacation trip west, Dad had the car checked over and had bought four new tires.

On the second day on the road a rear tire blew. The family was jolted severely, and Dad barely kept the car on the highway as he brought it to a halt.

Dad got out of the car and four-year-old Nadine followed him. Shaken, Mom and two-year-old Ellen remained inside. Dad said nothing as he simply stood back and looked at the tire. It was literally in shreds, the cords broken and tangled, pieces of tread hanging askew from the main body of the tire.

Nadine spoke first, "Daddy, can you put the tire back together again?"

Still gazing in disbelief and not looking up, Dad replied deliberately, "Sweetie, all the king's horses and all the king's men couldn't put that tire back together."

Dad removed the wheel and replaced it with the spare as Nadine watched and jabbered. Finally he lowered the jack, replaced the tools and wiped his hands as best he could on the roadside weeds. He and Nadine got in the car; he started the engine and pulled cautiously into the line of traffic.

"I can't get over it," he commented, "a brand new tire."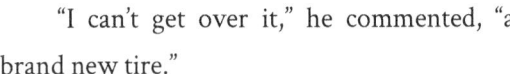

"What kind of a tire is it?" Mom asked.

Nadine jumped in with the necessary information:

"It's a Humpty Dumpty tire, Mom!"

BETTER THAN STARVING

When Chuckie was eight, he went with his parents to Grandfather's house for Thanksgiving dinner. There were several desserts, and it happened that a jellyroll, cut into nine slices, was placed directly in front of the youngster.

After the main course, the child consumed two slices of the roll and was reaching for a third. His mother fidgeted a bit and made a move as though to restrain him and passed the jellyroll to others. As she did so, she felt a gentle hand on her arm, then looked into Grandfather's face which, by its expression, seemed to be saying, "No, no, don't stop the boy; let's watch this!"

After his third piece, the boy took a fourth, and then a fifth. The others talking and laughing, seemed oblivious to this scene near the end of the table where Grandpa now had a gay twinkle in his eye, and Mother had relaxed and given into the plot.

The child reached for a sixth piece; a slowing of his performance was now discernible, but just barely.

Then number seven.

When he took his eighth, he sighed, then picked up his fork. It appeared that the boy had in truth reached his capacity. He finished, wiped his mouth with his napkin, folded his arms and sat back.

Grandfather quickly looked away, giving the impression of being deeply engrossed in the conversation of the others. A minute or two passed, then he turned his attention to the youngster obviously eyeing the remaining slice and asked, "What's the matter, Chuckie, didn't you care for the jellyroll?"

"Well, it was all right," came the reply, "but I don't really like that kind of jelly!"

BIBLE LESSON

Returning home from church, one of the Schultz children asked, "What are we having for dinner, Mom?"

"We're having liver and onions," the mother replied.

"Oh," said Chuckie, the youngest. "We talked about that in Sunday School this morning."

"You did?" asked the surprised mother, "How did that come up?"

"It was part of a prayer we were learning."

"A prayer? What prayer?"

"I think it's called the Lord's Prayer."

"But what does liver and onions have to do with it?"

"It says right in the prayer, 'liver us from evil.'"

BIG HELP TO DAD

The Harper family often went to auctions and garage sales with their eight-year-old son, Donny.

One night the Harpers had Mr. and Mrs. Foster as dinner guests. Now, Mr. Foster was Mr. Harper's employer, and he was so introduced to Donny, but the lad's mind evidently was drifting at the time of the introduction, a supposition that seemed to be born out by the child's remark when Mrs. Foster questioned him at the dinner table.

The conversation had evolved around to the discussion of the "bargains" that the Harpers occasionally snapped up at the sales.

Seeking to draw young Donny into the conversation, Mrs. Foster asked, "Donny, do you also like going to auctions?"

"Yeah, sometimes, I guess."

"Well, it sounds like your mother and dad make some good buys when they go."

"Yeah, I suppose so. My dad says he has to save all the money he can cause he works for a real cheap outfit!"

BIG TOP SUPER MARKET

Mom and three-year-old Suzanne remained in the car while Dad ran into the supermarket to pick up a couple of items. He was gone a long time and when he returned to the car, Mom asked, "You only had to get bread and eggs. How come you were gone so long?"

"Wow," he replied, "there were huge lines in there, people, people all over the place."

When they arrived home, Suzanne went directly to the phone and she was heard to report to her friend, "Hey, Judy, my dad was just in the grocery store and there were some great big lions in there!"

BLABBER MOUTH

Grandpa had to run to town with his pickup truck to get the lawn mower fixed, and Naomi, age six, asked to go along.

"Okay with me," Grandpa said, "but you go check with your grandma."

"Certainly you can go if you wear your seat belt," Grandma said.

The trip to town was uneventful with everybody buckled up.

The mower was fixed and loaded in the truck, and the pair hopped in to return home. Grandpa buckled up, then sat there making no move to start the engine.

"What are you waiting for, Grandpa?" the child asked.

"I'm waiting for you to buckle up. Darned if I'm going to get into trouble with your grandma."

Part way home the child decided to open the back window and to do so she unfastened her belt, and turning again to face forward, made no move to refasten the belt.

"Hey, young lady, you get that belt fastened or your grandma won't ever let you go with me again."

The child fastened the belt, then was silent for a minute or more. "Hey, Grandpa," she finally asked, "Haven't you ever learned to keep your mouth shut?"

BOOB TUBE ADDICT

Four-year-old Ben was supposed to be having his nap. His father, a newspaper feature writer, was working in an adjacent room.

Instead of napping, the youngster was reading to his teddy bear. "Reading" in this case consisted of pointing to the pictures and explaining what they portrayed.

"This is a butterfly and he is sucking the sweet juice out of the flower."

"This is a robin and he's digging up a worm for his supper."

"This is a frog. He's sitting on the lily pad to sun himself."

At this point Ben found it necessary to excuse himself. He closed the book and laid it on the bed.

As he slid off the bed he turned to face the teddy bear, "I have to go to the bathroom," he said "but don't go away I'll be right back after these messages!"

BORROWED TIME

A friend was flying from Chicago to Denver and happened to be seated next to a small boy traveling alone. The youngster was very talkative and was especially anxious to explain to my friend the device he held in his hand.

"This is an inhalator. I have to carry it with me all the time. I have asthma. Asthma is a very serious sickness. I use the inhalator when I have an asthma attack. I use it like this to spray medical vapors into my nasal passages," the boy said, demonstrating. "It's very important that I am never without my inhalator. If I didn't have the inhalator I could even die."

"That's interesting," my friend said, "especially interesting to me because my son has asthma."

"How old is your son?"

"Oh, he's a grown man now, he's thirty-two."

"You mean he's not dead yet?"

BROKEN RECORD

Jim and Bob's parents are unusually good in giving their children adequate and reasonable explanations when denying requests and requiring certain conduct.

The crappies were finally hitting as the long weekend drew to a close. It was time to pull up anchor and quit fishing, but, "Aw, please, Dad, just a little while longer," had prevailed, partly, of course, because Dad also enjoyed pulling in the green and black speckled beauties.

But finally the time for departure could not be postponed any longer. Darkness was approaching, and there was no flashlight in the boat. Back at the island, the fish would have to be cleaned and the cabin closed. The family would have to pack the boat and head for mainland, transfer all to the car and drive the forty miles to their home. There would have to be baths as there was school the next day.

All this the boys surely knew, but gee! When the crappies are biting?

And all this, too, the father was prepared to patiently explain, so to the next "Aw, please, Dad—" he began:

"Well, now look boys—"

At this point, Jim turned to his brother, "Uh, oh, Bob," he said, "here we go again with the logic stuff!"

BROTHER TO THE RESCUE

Jerry and George were twins. In many characteristics they were much alike, but when it came to orderliness they were as far apart as the poles.

Mom was constantly picking up after George and was not backward about expressing her annoyance.

It was after an especially exasperating, hot, humid, July day. Hoping for a relaxing evening of television, she went to the den only to find wall-to-wall disorder, clothes, school papers and sports equipment everywhere.

She exploded, "George, I swear, I do swear, I'm going to get a rope and I'm going to hang you from the nearest tree."

At this point Jerry, put in his two cents' worth.

"Don't do it till Sunday, Mom. It's his turn to mow the lawn tomorrow!"

BRUTAL LETDOWN

Todd's class had been studying prehistoric animals and he became fascinated with dinosaurs.

Often a child gets on a "kick" regarding a given subject, wherein, for a short time, he will eat, sleep and prattle about that which has captured his interest.

Todd wanted his dad to take him to the library so he could learn more about this creature which was, perhaps only temporarily, his favorite animal.

Then, at the dinner table, it was: "Dinosaurs weren't all huge like most people think. There were a great many species of dinosaurs and some were no bigger than a dog. Still, some dinosaurs weighed as much as eighty tons and stood so high they could eat the leaves from the tops of tall trees.

"Scientists think dinosaurs became extinct in a short time rather than over a long period of time. They think something happened like maybe a large meteorite – that's a shooting star – striking the earth which caused a huge dust cloud that blocked out the sun's rays, causing vegetation to die, and then the animals starved.

"Scientists say dinosaurs were ancestors of some animals still living today, even our birds."

Dinosaurs this— dinosaurs that—

At the very height of Todd's fascination with dinosaurs, he heard, and thus informed his parents that there was to be a dinosaur show on television. Would his parents watch it with him? Yes, they would. It was to be shown at 7:30 p.m. Todd phoned all his school buddies and told them the time and station. This was, indeed, to be the pinnacle of his pursuit of knowledge about the ancient dinosaur.

Todd was sitting before the tube at 7:20, calling the others to come, lest they miss part of the show.

With avid interest he glued his eyes on the screen.

The next day, Todd didn't mention dinosaurs.

During the TV presentation, a pretty lady had come forth and sung some songs.

This was entirely fitting because it was the Dinah Shore Show!

BUSINESS ACUMEN

After several requests, Jim's father brought home a very large inner tube. He placed it on the lawn and called the boy who was ecstatic and began jumping on it as though it were a trampoline.

Dad then went to his desk and became absorbed in paper work. Later Jim came in and excitedly told about his fun with the new plaything. The child noticed a picture in his father's wastebasket and asked if he could have it.

"Yes, sure, you can always have anything that's in my waste basket."

Soon the child spied a set of new color markers on top of the desk and picked them up one by one to examine them. A purple marker especially appealed to him. "Can I have this, Dad?"

"Well, it's not a toy, you'll have to pay for it. Let's see, it cost me, well, about seven cents. You'll have to pay me seven cents for it."

Jim put the marker back with the others and left.

After about an hour he was back and offered a nickel and two pennies for the purple marker.

Now Dad was in the habit of emptying his loose change on top of his dresser, and he knew Jim was out of funds because that very morning it had been noted that he had squandered all his allowance on M&Ms, and the week was not yet half over.

Dad looked accusingly at Jim and demanded, "Jimmy, let me see what's in your other hand."

The lad seemed frightened but opened the other hand. It held an assortment of pennies, nickels and dimes.

Immediately Dad's voice became even more threatening. "James, exactly where did you get that money?"

Jim began to cry.

"I – I – I – charged the k – k – kids a penny a jump to jump on my inner tube!"

CHECKS AND BALANCES

When Marvin first learned the truth about the jolly little elf of Christmastime, it was as if his whole world had come crashing down around him.

"You lied to me," he accused his parents. "Why did you lie?"

"It's sort of a game," his father replied, "most everyone enjoys it. You enjoyed it, didn't you?" There was no reply.

Marvin's most frequent infringement was in the area of food. To him, meringue on a pie, the frosting on a cake, or any reasonably exact facsimile thereof, was irresistible.

It was, perhaps, a month after the Santa exposé that Marvin's mother had made a three-layer cake for expected company. The frosting which she had heaped on top was chocolate, another devastating pitfall for Marvin. She had intended to put the cake out of his reach but the phone rang and she became absorbed in conversation. She stood aghast when she returned to the kitchen!

She greatly feared her own mounting anger, refrained from uttering even a word, deciding to lay the whole case before her husband when he would arrive home.

"Marvin," he began, "haven't you been told time after time to get permission before eating any food between meals?"

"Yes, sir."

"And haven't you been told time after time never to touch special food prepared for a special occasion?"

"Yes, sir."

"And didn't you know when you scooped the frosting off that cake that your aunt and cousins were coming for dinner tonight, and that the cake was our dessert?"

"Yes, sir."

"Well, then, don't you think you should be punished?"

"No, sir."

"No? Well, why not?"

"Because after all those times I was being good because you had me believing there was a Santa Claus, it seems like I ought to be allowed to be bad once in a while now that I know there isn't any!"

CHOSEN CAREER

When Grandma asked Jerry where his older brother was, he replied, "He's outside playing batsball with the big guys."

Grandma impulsively grabbed the youngster and, with a squeeze, said, "Oh, you little bum."

It had come to be a habit, this grabbing the three-year-old whenever he did or said something cute, chuckling softly while giving him an affectionate hug, and saying, "Oh you little bum!"

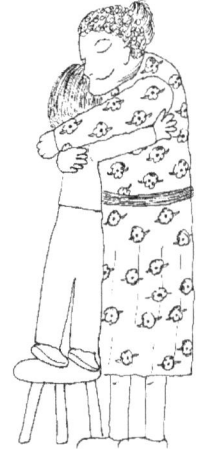

One day Jerry asked, "Grandma, what's a bum?"

"Oh, a bum," she replied, "is someone who won't work, just wants to lay around and do nothing. Maybe he even begs for food because he's too lazy to work for it. Maybe he's dirty and too lazy to shave, his clothes are dirty, maybe even torn and ragged." She chuckled that soft chuckle and again pulled him to her with an affectionate squeeze. "You're a little bum," she said, tightening her hug and laughing so that there could be no mistaking the fact that she called him a bum in loving fun.

As the lad grew, the habit continued whenever Grandma came to visit. Finally Jerry entered kindergarten, and one day the teacher reported the following to Jerry's mother: She had asked the children what they wanted to be when they grew up. When it came Jerry's turn he stated, "I want to be a bum."

"A bum?" I asked; I guess I showed my surprise. "Why on earth would you want to be a bum?"

"Because it gets me nice hugs from my grandma!"

CHRISTMAS DINNER

Justin's father was an avid hunter and fisherman. He started taking his son, Justin, fishing with him when the lad was only three, and hunting when he was four. Of course the boy did no actual shooting, but his father always spoke of "we" in connection with their exploits. "'We' caught an eight pounder." "'We' got our limit on pheasants." When the game was cleaned, Justin always looked on, learning, and occasionally actually helping.

During the week before Christmas, it was necessary for Dad to go out of town on business. When he returned, he brought with him a pair of parakeets as a gift for his older daughter, Tammy. His return was late at night, and the children were in bed. He spread newspapers on the kitchen table and set the bird cage on them, then hit the sack.

When he arose the next morning and went into the kitchen, he found Justin peering at the birds. The boy looked up at his father and asked, "When we gonna clean 'em, Dad?"

CLOCK WATCHER

Carrie's aunt, uncle and cousins were visiting; although the hour was getting late, she was enjoying the chitchat and lingered with the group.

She yawned a couple of times and finally asked, "What time is it?"

Her cousin asked, "Why do you want to know?"

"Cuz, I want to know if I'm tired yet!"

CLOTHES MAKE THE MAN

Jennifer was six days old. At age three, Michael was awed by the newcomer. There was so much mystery about the whole thing. When he had been told the baby was "in Mommy's tummy," the concept was beyond him. Now, seeing the living flesh, the tiny fingers and toes, the wiggling, and hearing the crying, overwhelmed him.

There was a special sort of table set up in the bathroom, and Michael, peeking through the door, saw his mother changing the baby's diaper.

Later that day, Michaels's friend, Terry, came to the house and he was allowed to see the baby, after which, Michael was heard explaining to his friend, "I think it's another Jesus."

"Jesus?" Terry asked in amazement, "How come you think it's another Jesus?"

"'Cuz, my mom was wrapping it in swaddling clothes!"

COFFEE BREAK

Kendra at age four had not previously attended church when communion was served. She was invited by a friend to attend the latter's church, and when she returned home her mother asked her about the experience.

"Did you enjoy attending church with Kathie?"

"Yeah, it was fun."

"Was it like our church?"

"Well, sort of."

"How was it different from ours?"

"They served sandwiches and Kool-Aid!"

COMMENT ON AGING

Eddie was only six years old when his much older brother married and became a father. The boy had heard talk about his (Eddie's) parents becoming grandparents and the relationships between the baby and other family members.

Eddie was allowed to go to the hospital and view the newcomer through a window. On the way home his father asked, "Well, Eddie, how do you like being an uncle?"

The child seemed to be in deep thought for a moment, then, "Well, I guess it's all right. I guess I'd rather be an uncle than a grandpa!"

COME ON, TEACH, BE EXPLICIT

"Friday, this next Friday is Father's Night," the teacher announced. "We want you all to bring your fathers to school for this event. We do this once a semester and it's very important that each of you come and bring your father." (Note the exact wording of what the teacher said as this is crucial to our story.)

Freddie reported to his father, "Dad, I'm supposed to take you to school Friday night, it's called Father's Night, but, gee…"

"But, gee, what?" his father asked.

"Well, I don't know…"

"What kind of trouble do you suppose he's in?" his father said to Freddie's mother when they were alone.

"I haven't the foggiest notion. I've had no inkling of anything being wrong."

Each time Father's Night was mentioned, the child seemed extremely nervous, and on Friday he seemed almost ill. At dinner time he had no appetite and when Father's Night was mentioned, he blurted out, "I don't want to go!"

"Oh, but we must go," his father said. "It's very important. Why don't you want to go?"

"Well, I want to go, but—"

"But what? You want to go, but what?"

The child broke into tears, "Well, I want to go, but I don't know how to drive!"

COMPANY POLICY!

There was an offensive odor in the classroom. Supposedly the school was cleaned over the weekend but on Monday the odor was even worse. The principal was summoned and then the custodian, and the final diagnosis was that a mouse or rat had died somewhere within the walls.

The children were advised of this and Lucas evidently grasped certain essentials of the story and related to his parents only that "a rat had come to the school and was causing an awful stink."

A few days later, Lucas's mother came to school and as soon as she entered the classroom, she said, "Oh, my goodness, that is an awful smell.

That rat must still be with you."

"Yeah," Lucas responded, "he's not-returnable!"

COMPARTMENTALIZED STORAGE

Beth's parents had allowed their child's sweet tooth to get out of hand. A more healthy diet had slowly given way to the child's preference for candy, cake, ice cream, cookies, etc. Meat, potatoes, vegetables, salads were often left on her plate uneaten.

Mom and Dad finally realized it was time for a showdown.

At dinner the first night under the new program, Dad served onto Beth's plate, balanced portions of meat, potatoes and vegetables. He was careful to limit the servings but, as usual, she stopped eating with almost half the food remaining on her plate.

Dad knew that there were chocolate pudding and cookies in the kitchen, ready to be served as dessert, and he knew that Beth knew.

"Come on now, Beth," he said, "finish your supper."

"I'm full, Daddy."

"You're full?"

"Yes."

"Now you're sure you're full?"

"Yes, I'm sure I'm full," but even as she finished the sentence, a strange expression crept over her face, as though it had suddenly struck her that by being so definite she had walked into a trap.

No more was said. Mom and Beth's older sister, Clara, cleared the table. As the two returned, Beth realized disaster had struck. Clara carried her own dessert and Mom carried two, setting one before her husband and the other at her own place.

Beth began to cry, and, of course, no one needed to ask why.

"But, Beth," her father said in a kind manner, "you said you were full. I asked you a second time, just so there would be no mistake, and you said you were sure."

"Well, I know," the child said between sobs. "My meat and potatoes compartment is full, and my vegetable compartment is full, but there's lots of room left in my dessert compartment."

COMPREHENSIVE COVERAGE

It was February, and the class had studied the lives of both Washington and Lincoln. Later they were asked to write a paragraph on something they had learned about either of the presidents.

Little Florence had been absent during part of the sessions, but she had heard some of the other children discussing the material; her paragraph read as follows:

"George Washington was a nice man, but he cut down a cherry tree, so when he went to President Ford's theater, somebody shot him!"

COMPUTER AGE

Six-year-old Joey was driving to Duluth with his grandfather. When they neared the city and slowed for the first stop light, the child said, "Grandpa, this is where that accident was that we saw when we came down here last year, remember?"

Grandpa thought for a minute, then said slowly, as though he was still deliberating, "No, Joey, I guess I don't remember that."

After a few seconds' pause, the child spoke, "Well, I suppose you have a lot on your mind and you've reprogrammed over that already, but I still have more space left in my RAM!"

CONDITIONED APPETITE

At the orphanage, the fare consisted of meat and potatoes, bread and butter, fruit and vegetables. No caviar antipasto, no Quiche Lorraine, no pâté de foie gras.

The adoption was finalized; Kelly Jo would live with the Marshalls. Needless to say, it was a busy day, introducing the child to her new home, putting away her few belongings, neighbors coming to meet the new member of the family. Time slipped away.

Finally the new family was alone. It was after five o'clock.

"Well," Mrs. Marshall said, "I've got to get organized for dinner."

"Mrs. Marshall," Kelly Jo suggested, "couldn't we just have meat and potatoes, I don't think I'd like organized!"

CONSIDERATE STUDENT

Marsha, a former Montessori student returned for a visit after a few weeks in public school.

"Well, Marsha," her former teacher asked, "How do you like public school?"

"Oh, it's all right I guess."

"What are you studying right now?"

"Oh, in reading we're studying three letter words."

"Oh, that ought to be real easy for you; we did all that long ago, didn't we?"

"Yeah, we did and it is easy, but I try not to let my teacher know. She's real nice, and I don't want to hurt her feelings!"

CREATIVE THINKING

Christina showed up in school all bruised and scarred.

"Mercy, mercy, what happened to you?" the teacher asked.

"I was riding my bicycle, and my shoelaces got caught in the sprocket, and I went head over heels," the child responded.

"Well," the teacher said brightly, "from every experience, good or bad, we learn something, don't we?"

"Yeah, I sure did!"

"Well, why don't you tell the class what you learned from this unpleasant accident," the teacher asked.

Mentally the teacher reviewed the possibilities – wear shorter shoelaces, tie the laces more securely, wear sandals when biking, etc.

"I learned that when you ride your bike," Christina reported, "you should go barefooted!"

CURRENT CONCERN

After his older brother had received a severe shock when experimenting with an electrical outlet, something the boys had been warned not to do, Mark was consumed with curiosity about electricity.

One day his mother was getting dressed and she casually remarked, "Oh, these hose are just full of electricity."

She pulled the stockings on and continued to get dressed. Mark watched her rather intently, as though he expected something unusual to occur, then finally he said:

"Mom, would I get a shock if I put my finger in your belly button?"

DEFINITELY NOT IRISH SETTER

Jeff heard a good deal of talk about animals since his father was a veterinarian, and he had also seen all varieties of species of pets in his father's waiting room. This, coupled with the fact that the lad was only three, seems ample excuse for a slight faux pas in his vocabulary.

His mother had taken him to the doctor, and in the waiting room there was an Asian child about Jeff's age and size, also waiting with his mother.

As Jeff was sitting quietly, the Asian boy approached and touched him on the knee, then moved on giving his attention to other people and things in the room. He made the rounds, so to speak, and soon was back and touched Jeff again and jabbered a bit, then moved on, then again came back to Jeff.

Jeff, a bit shy, was slow to speak, but he had taken note of the oriental features, and finally spoke up, asking, "Are you Pekinese or what?"

DEPUTIZED PARENT

It was to be a happy day. Tania's mother had promised she would take the child to the carnival when it came to town, and today was the day. "We'll go and we'll stay as long as you're having fun," the mother said.

The child was enchanted with the clowns and amused by the monkeys and thrilled by the cotton candy that she managed to spread from ear to ear and bangs to chin.

Then came the pony ride, which is where the trouble started. Mom stepped up to the booth and paid the two-dollar fee, then said to Tania, "Now, Honey, you take this ticket and go get in that line right over there." The child burst into tears, refused to take the ticket, and started running.

Bewildered, the mother ran after the child who eluded her and was crying almost hysterically. When the mother finally caught up and grabbed her daughter's arm, the child squirmed and writhed, "I don't want to go to jail, I don't want to go to jail!" the child cried.

"Jail? Jail? Honey, what are you talking about?"

"You tried to give me a ticket. I don't want a ticket, cause then I'd have to go to jail!"

DESERT SONGS

As a mid-westerner, Florence's first trip through the west and southwest brought her many sights and experiences to be remembered. Other than Disneyland, that which left the greatest impression on the child was the desert flowers. By chance, the family drove through cactus country after a heavy rain which brought out the blooms in magnificent splendor and profusion.

The child cherished this memory and looked forward to reporting the experience in school. When she did so, she fairly glowed as she relived the moments when she viewed the blossoming cactuses. When she had finished, the teacher said, "Very good, Florence, that was a fine report and you made us see and share your delightful experience. Now tell us, you have described the beauty of the cacti, but can you tell us in what other ways these desert plants serve mankind?"

The child thought a moment. "Well," she replied rather hesitatingly, "well, I think there is cactus candy, and some have fruit."

"Fine, now are there any other ways?" The teacher was thinking of the plants that store water and have been known to save the lives of those thirsting in the hot desert. "Something very important to man," she added.

The child seemed puzzled for a moment, then she brightened, "Oh, yes, I remember, there's one that they make pipe organs out of!"

DESSERT—NO EXTRA CHARGE

Georgia, at age five, was bugging her father, "Daddy, Shirley says their family goes to Ming's Chinese Restaurant, and the food is just wonderful. Can we go there, Daddy?"

The plea was repeated and finally Dad gave in and on a Friday night took the family to Ming's.

Georgia's friend had talked about the almond Chicken Chop Suey, so Georgia promptly ordered it. Her parents and her older brother, Tom, studied the menu a bit and then made their selections.

After Georgia took her first bite she exclaimed, "Oh boy, is this good. I just love it!" A moment later she again commented enthusiastically. Then, "Mommy, isn't this just wonderful?"

"Really very good," her mother replied.

"Daddy, isn't this food great?"

"Terrible, just terrible," her father responded, grinning.

Joining the tease, Tom commented, "Gee, mine's just awful; I think it's going to make me sick!"

In addition to relishing the food, Georgia enjoyed the teasing and kept it going by using all the derogatory terms she could think of to describe the male animal!

The meal over, the check paid, the family headed home in the car. The banter continued, and amid much giggling and laughing, Georgia continued to praise the food and her father and brother found all the expressions they could to knock it.

Finally the hilarity ebbed and the group drove quietly. Suddenly Georgia gave out a resounding "burp!" There were a few seconds of silence, then:

"Gee, you guys, even when I belch it tastes good!"

DEVILISH ANGEL

Pattie was the mischievous type, never intentionally destructive, but ever seeking to tease or bring off a four-year-old's version of a practical joke. Even though her seven-year-old brother, Bobby, was sometimes a victim, he at other times was often a co-conspirator.

Grief devastated Bobby and his parents when Pattie separated from them at this tender age. To know all of the boy's inner thoughts regarding the tragedy was, of course impossible, but his father got a glimpse of at least one facet of the boy's reflections a week or so after the funeral services. They were riding in the car. The sky had been overcast all day, but suddenly the rain came; and it came heavily and in large drops.

As the boy began to speak, his father glanced over at him. Now, thirty years later, he, the father, stresses his recollection of the angelic expression he observed on the lad's face as he said solemnly,

"Pattie's up there in heaven, punching holes in the clouds!"

DIABOLICAL RUMOR

Resentment in an older child when a new baby comes along occurs frequently, and this phenomenon is mentioned in other stories in this book.

In this case, however, the newcomer was not yet in existence. As a matter of fact, Mommy was still "skinny as a rail."

The sitter for two-and-a-half-year-old Gracie was not in on all the family secrets, but, of course, in this modern age, the discovery of the pregnancy was not concealed from the child.

One morning, the sitter called Gracie's mother and said she'd like to come over, that she had a matter to discuss.

"Mrs. Land, I hardly know how to begin, but there is something I think I should tell you."

Her demeanor was such as to suggest that something serious was about to be mentioned. "What on earth is it?" Mrs. Land asked anxiously.

"Now, of course, I don't know whether or not it's true. I certainly haven't seen any evidence that it is, but I did think I ought to mention it to you and let you check out the matter as you see fit."

"Well, what is it? What's the problem?"

"Well, Gracie tells me, and insists it's true, that her daddy has been beating her."

Mrs. Land's mouth dropped open in unbelief. Very soon, her face relaxed, "Oh, that's not true, I just know that's not true. Andy adores that child. There just can't possibly be a word of truth in it."

She went to the door. "Gracie, you come here," she called.

The child came, seemed a bit surprised to see Mrs. Willis, the sitter. "What Mom?"

"Gracie, what have you been telling Mrs. Willis?"

"Nothing."

Mrs. Land raised her voice, "Gracie, I want to know what this is that you've been telling Mrs. Willis."

"Nothing."

"It's about your daddy beating you, Gracie," Mrs. Willis volunteered. "You've been telling me that he beat you several times."

"No, I didn't. I didn't tell you that."

"Yes you did, and you told me several times."

"Now, Gracie," Mrs. Land demanded, "I want to know the meaning of this. Why have you been telling this lie about your daddy?"

Now sobbing, the child declared, "Well, I just wanted to get even. We don't want any old baby in this house and Daddy went and planted one in your tummy!"

DID HE CHECK THE RADIATOR?

When Dora had had a baby tooth pulled, it had hurt only a little, but she was aware of the stories that other more complicated dental work can be very painful. She had heard, too, that dentists often "give something" for the pain, even sometimes making patients unconscious by giving them "gas." This all seemed pretty frightening to her, so she was apprehensive when her father complained of a very severe toothache and had to go to the dentist.

"Daddy," she asked when he returned home with a swollen cheek, "did it hurt?"

"Yes, some."

"Did he give you something for the pain?"

"Oh, yes."

"Wha'd he give you, oil or gas?"

DISCONTENTED COWS?

Although at four years of age, Paula was too young to grasp many of the details of cooking, her mother did encourage the child to watch and "work along" with her on the theory that her daughter would learn by doing and watching, and come to feel at home with kitchen tasks.

Thus it was that at Thanksgiving dinner, Paula was overheard telling her cousin how she and her mother had made the pumpkin pie that was soon to be served.

"We beat up the eggs and then stirred them together with the sugar and pumpkin and spices, and then finally we added and stirred in the exasperated milk!"

DISPOSING OF THE RIFF RAFF

It is not unusual when a first child resents, consciously or unconsciously, the arrival of a second child. Jeff never really accepted Paul who arrived when he, Jeff, was two, but up until the time the baby was about ten months old, there had been no physical violence.

However, one day when Mother was busy with housework, she heard water running. The noise was just vaguely on the edge of her attention, and she assumed Jeff had flushed the toilet. Suddenly, however, she realized that the water was continuing to run.

As she approached the bathroom, she heard giggling mixed with the sound of steadily running water.

Aghast, she found Paul in the toilet, Jeff holding the flush lever down and an expression on the older boy's face which seemed to be saying, "Heck, why won't he go down?"

DIVISION OF LABOR

The preschoolers went on a field trip to a large dairy farm in a nearby town. Here the children saw large numbers of cows grazing in the meadow, then went into the barn where they witnessed the animals being milked by modern milking equipment. Next they were taken on into the pasteurizing area, the cooling area, and finally into the packaging room. Each process was explained by the guide.

Then, each child was given a small carton of milk and some cookies. Marcie, who was barely four, opened her carton of milk and peered inside but left the milk untouched. Before the group was dismissed, the guide asked if there were any questions.

Marcie held up her hand, the guide nodded, "Yes, young lady, what is it?"

"Could we go see the chocolate cows?"

DO THAT ONE AGAIN, GRANDPA

The main thing that Carl, now six, remembered about his grandfather was that he did magic tricks. Two years ago on Grandfather's previous visit, he entertained with sleight of hand which was not, to an adult, particularly sophisticated, but, to the lad, was entertaining and deeply mystifying.

Carl could not remember the specifics of the tricks, but his first question to the elder when the family met him at the airport was, "Hey, Grampa, ya got any new tricks?"

"No, nothing new," Grandpa answered chuckling, "but we can do a rerun on the old ones."

Carl was able to wait, but not patiently, while his parents visited and snacked with Grandpa for an hour or more prior to the magic show.

Grandpa ran through his legerdemain as Carl watched entranced. Then, tired from his long trip, Grandpa said he'd like to hit the sack.

Carl, still excited by the arrival of his grandfather as well as the magic show, followed him into his room and continued to chatter.

"Carl," the boy's mother called, "you come on and leave Grandpa alone. He's tired and wants to go to bed, and it's time for you to turn in too."

"Yeah, Mom, pretty soon."

After another few minutes, his mother had to call him again, and again the boy agreed but stalled.

Then suddenly he came bouncing excitedly out of the room and into the den where his parents were. "Grandpa did too learn a new trick," the child exclaimed. "He took his teeth right out of his mouth!"

DOUBLE CROSSED

When, at age ten, Stephanie learned that her married sister was to have a baby, the child ranted and stormed.

"Mother," she charged, "you told me I'd always be your little baby. When Heidi's brat is born you won't look at me anymore. I'll tell you one thing: that darn kid won't get anything off of me. I'm going to be the meanest aunt that ever lived!"

She was kidding, of course, and enjoying the attention her show commanded. Still, she was dropping a hint, veiled in her own little brand of humor, that she did not expect to be ignored, once the newcomer arrived.

When she heard that Heidi had had a boy, she put on another performance. Bad enough that any baby should encroach on her territory, but a boy? Ugh!

Then came the day that the baby was left with his grandmother. "Stephanie," her mother commented matter-of-factly, "it looks to me as though you need a lot of practice." The youngster took a quick assessment: the infant was adequately clad; she was supporting his head properly; he seemed perfectly satisfied, in fact was even cooing as Stephanie danced around the room with him.

"Why, what am I doing wrong?" she asked puzzled.

"Nothing wrong, that's just it. You need to do a whole lot of practicing at being mean."

The child's face took on a perplexed, then an embarrassed and caught-in-the-act expression, and there was a note of defiance in her manner and voice as she blurted, "Well, gosh, how did I know he was going to be so darn cute?"

DRINKING PROBLEM

On a visit to grandmother's house, Andrew was making himself at home with the refrigerator. He had downed Coke after Coke and was now on his fourth.

His mother admonished him, "Andrew, for heaven's sake, you're drinking Coke like it was water. Now that's enough, no more!" she said emphatically.

The child looked puzzled for a moment, but soon expressed his willingness to reform. "Okay, if I drink it like Coke, can I have some more?"

DULY EDUCATED PARENTS

The boys had been sparring with the girls.

"Boy, you girls are for the birds," said seven-year-old Tom, "I'm sure glad I'm a boy. I'm sure never going to get married to a girl."

"Me too," nine-year-old Max added, "I'm gonna be a bachelor."

Nine-year-old Lester, a newcomer to the neighborhood, put in his contribution. "Me, too, I'm gonna be a bachelor like my dad."

Immediately, Tom's mother perked up her ears. "Your father's a bachelor, Lester?" she asked in shocked amazement.

"Yeah."

"But, I've met your mother, she lives with you and your dad, doesn't she?"

"Yeah, sure."

"Then, what do you mean, your dad's a bachelor?"

"Well, my dad and mom are both bachelors. I've heard 'em talk about it lots of times. They went to the same college, and they got be Bachelors of Art!"

DUPLICITY IN ACTION

The Montessori school was on an acreage where a few farm implements as well as animals were kept. It became tradition that at the annual picnic, the school mistress' husband gave all the children a ride on the tractor. At the tender age of four, twin sisters Lauren and Michele had already mastered the art of using their twin-hood as a conning tool and were using it to get extra rides ("That was my sister who just got off."). It eventually dawned on Mr. George, the tractor driver, that some of his passengers were look-alikes and that it was he who had been taken for a ride.

So when one of the twins again started to climb aboard, he said to her (Lauren or Michele—he'll never know which), "Don't you think you and your sister have had your share of rides? Don't you think it would be nice to let some of the other kids ride?"

It was then that this little four-year-old angel, pink bows on her pigtails, delicate lace on the collar and cuffs of her blouse, a sweet, mysterious fragrance issuing forth from her person, turned and said:

"How would you like me to punch your face out?"

EASY SHOPPING

The teacher had noticed that Siri, a cute three-year-old girl, always wore becoming clothes. One morning she appeared wearing a sweater with a hippopotamus on it. (To quote the teacher, "It was darling!")

"Siri," the teacher asked, "Where does your mom find all your cute clothes?"

There was no hesitation with the response, "In my closet!"

EATING FOR TWO

Toby was four when his mother discovered that the lad was to have a little brother or sister. June was Mom's fifth month and, inasmuch as she was not doing too well, Toby's grandparents offered to take him to their farm for the summer. The child enjoyed being in the country and became familiar with the farm routines as well as many of the expressions used by farm folk. Although Mom and Dad, and the grandparents as well, spoke of the fact that Toby was to have a new brother or sister, no one went into detail, and the child never asked where the baby was to come from.

He returned home in late August and the pregnancy was now three months further along. Mom greeted him with a big hug, and then the child stood back, and his gaze went from Mom's head to her toes.

"Gee, Mom," the boy said, "you sure have been puttin' on the feed bag, haven't cha?"

ELECTRO-MAGIC

It was now two weeks after Christmas, and five-year-old Freddie's little robot, which was named Fetchit, wouldn't work. "Daddy," the lad said, "Fetchit's broken. Will you fix him for me?" The boy wouldn't let his dad alone till he had checked out the problem, and the diagnosis disclosed that Fetchit needed new batteries.

There was pressure to go out and get the needed batteries that very moment, but bedtime was at hand, and Dad was able to forestall the expedition till the next day.

After work, Dad duly accomplished his chore, arrived home, enjoyed dinner with the family, installed the batteries, and everything settled back to normal.

Freddie's three-year-old sister, Sandra, had overheard all the conversations, but was busy with her coloring book so had not actually witnessed the changing of batteries. By now, most of her Christmas crayons were broken, and she was coloring with the remaining short pieces.

When bedtime came and both children were told to put their playthings away, Sandra went to her father with a request.

"Daddy," she said, "all of my crayons are broken. When you come home tomorrow night, will you bring me some new batteries for my crayon set?"

EMERGENCY OPERATION

Mrs. George was three things: a good mother, a good teacher and a firm disciplinarian. Thus, when her six-year-old son, Charlie, moved from kindergarten into her first grade class, she resolved that he would be treated with no more leniency than any of her other pupils. As a matter of fact, bending over backwards so as not to favor him, she probably was stricter with him than his classmates. Too, knowing him better than the others, and aware that his quickness of mind augmented his bent for mischief, she often was able to anticipate and thwart an escapade in the making.

On a Saturday in late October, when Mrs. George took Charlie for his annual check-up, the youngster asked, "What's the doctor going to do, Mom?"

"Oh, he'll just check to see if you're okay—like if your nose is on straight, whether you have dishwater in your blood, or any of your gears need to be greased."

The child chuckled, but when the doctor entered the room Charlie showed that he had some ideas of his own. "Doctor," he asked, "can you take those two eyes out of the back of my mother's head?"

EMPTY THEATRE

A friend told me of this incident he observed in a shopping mall:

A very well-dressed lady was having a problem with her equally well-dressed little boy. He had thrown his hat on the floor in anger and was having a tantrum-like cry. The mother picked up the hat, placed it on the boy's head, saying, "Now you stop that crying this instant, and come along with me." The results she obtained were the same as though she'd been speaking to the planet Mars! The boy immediately grabbed the hat, threw it to the floor, then sat on the floor and continued his tantrum. Again the mother replaced the hat, pulled the boy to his feet and demanded that he come with her. Immediately there was a repeat performance—the whole bit.

With the hat on the floor, the boy sprawled and crying at the top of his lungs. The mother turned and walked down the hall, not looking back. The boy looked up and half stopped crying. The mother kept right on walking; now perhaps a hundred feet away, she made a right turn into the next hall, out of sight. The boy cast a quick look around, checking the audience. There wasn't any; I had pretended to look away. The crying ceased abruptly and completely. The boy rose to his feet, grabbed the hat, placed it neatly on his head, walked – no – ran down the hall, making the same turn his mother had made, and that was the end of that!

ENCORE

Jimmy had fallen head over heels down the cellar stairs. In their efforts to calm and console him, his parents had tried everything: pleading, petting, rocking. After a while, the father tried a new tack, declaring the tumble to be a great joke, doubling up with laughter. "Wasn't that great? Wasn't that fun?" he persisted.

It was several minutes before the sobs subsided, and then eventually there was a curl of the lips, ever so slight, which at long last broadened into a grin.

Finally, the child slowly wriggled from his mother's arms and stood up. At last, into his eyes crept a sly twinkle, and then:

"I'm gonna go do it again!"

ENERGY SHORTAGE

At age four, Edward had no understanding of the term "total eclipse," but when he learned that others were staying up late for a special event, he wanted to be included.

At the proper time, the family went out into the yard. It was a clear night, beautiful as the full moon illuminated the trees, lawns and houses which were interspersed with shadows.

From the conversation, Edward knew that the big light in the sky was the focal point of attention. He heard the adult and teenager talk as the dark crescent began, then increased its overlap of the glowing circle. Edward remained silent while the remarks of the others grew more intense and more excited.

The whole scene became darker now; the shadows faded, and then finally there was only a faint sliver of light, and then, just as this completely disappeared, the group fell silent.

It was then that Edward came forth with his appraisal of the event: "God needs new batteries for his flashlight!"

ENTREPRENEURIAL GENIUS

Prompted primarily by the desire to get his restless sons, Freddie, age five, and Jamie, seven, out of the house while he completed some work he had brought home for the weekend, and secondarily by an impulse for community improvement, Father offered the boys ten cents for each wagon load of litter they would pick up around the neighborhood.

In twenty minutes the boys were back, dumped their load in the family's trash container, collected ten cents and were off again. This time they were gone a bit longer, probably a half hour and again they collected their fee. Surprisingly, they were back fifteen minutes later with load number three, and, more surprisingly, the next load appeared even more quickly.

Back at his desk, Dad found his mind wandering. A vague thought was crossing his mind – a thought that became starkly real when his phone rang, he answered, and a voice said, "Mr. Baker, this is Cliff Walker down the block. Mr. Baker, I'm not complaining; I don't care, but curiosity is getting the best of me. Why are your boys taking junk out of my trash container?"

ESTABLISHED TECHNIQUE

It was at the family reunion; the adult siblings' practice of ribbing each other had become contagious, and the grandchildren did their best to compete.

It appeared that nine-year-old Charley was awaiting a chance to make his contribution. He had no rehearsal time, however, and displayed instant wit when his opportunity arrived.

Grandpa had just climbed into the boat to go out onto the lake and watch the moon rise. He handed Charley's dad a flashlight, saying, "Sometimes you have to slap that thing to make it work."

Quick as a flash, Charley zoomed in, "That's all right; my dad's good at that. He does that to my mom all the time to get her to work!"

ET CETERA, ET CETERA, ET CETERA

After my school teacher aunt's decease some years ago, the following was found among her papers:

As a teacher, I made a point of having the pupils know the words to important songs. It was Friday afternoon and Enrico's turn to recite. He stood and said:

My country, 'tis of thee,

Sweet Land of liberty,

Of thee I sing.

Land where my fathers died,

(pause)

Land where my mothers died,

Land where my babies cried,

To them I sing!

EVIDENCE IN: CASE CLOSED

Bo and Jessica were both bright children, three years of age, and they often engaged in a sort of intellectual competition. Thus when it was Jessica who first discovered that the Santa Claus, reindeer, chimney bit was a fraud perpetrated on the young she flaunted the information. Bo's reaction was vehement.

"There is too a Santa Claus!" he proclaimed emphatically.

"There is not!"

"There is so!"

"There is not!"

"There is so!"

"There is not!"

Finally Bo put his hands on his hips, leaned his trunk slightly forward, and dealt the devastation blow that would put the matter to rest, once and for all:

"Okay, Madam Know-It-All, then just tell me: who eats up those cookies and drinks up that milk?"

EXCESS BAGGAGE

In both amateur and professional psychology, the effect of a new baby upon an older child is a common subject for discussion. The idea of the new child elbowing the older out of the limelight is often real, especially to that older child.

But with Mark and Stewart, it was the other way around. Mark was only three and Stewart older by two years. They were normal siblings in that they were at times buddy-buddy, at other times anything but!

It was after one of the "anything but" episodes; the boys had been brawling, Mark, the younger and smaller, getting, as usual, the worst of the deal.

Mom came running and broke up the ruckus. She sent Stewart to his room and took Mark on her lap and rocked him a bit till the crying subsided. Then she took him to the bathroom and gently washed the mud from his face with warm water. This disclosed a few scratches, so she dipped some cotton in alcohol and dabbed it on the scratches. This brought forth another eruption of tears, and she again took him to the rocking chair.

Eventually the crying stopped and Mark laid silent and relaxed in her arms. Finally he stirred, looked his mother straight in the eye, and asked in a sober and sincere tone, "Mommy, why do we have Stewart?"

EXOTIC MORSEL

At the family reunion, much ado was made about the newest child, Peggy, who had just learned the art of crawling. All eyes were upon her after the picnic dinner as she demonstrated her new skill. She was on the green grass, crawling at a lively pace, giggling as she went.

Suddenly, she stopped dead still, seemed transfixed for a moment, then hurried on, grabbing at something ahead of her as she scrambled forward. Soon it dawned on the family watching her that a small frog was jumping on ahead of her. With each grab she would make, the frog made a leap, avoiding her clutch.

"Oooh," "aaah," and "oh isn't that just too darling for words?" were emanating from the assembly when suddenly the tiny hand slammed down and the frog was captured.

In a flash, the hand was at the mouth before anyone could even cry out a warning "no," Peggy swallowed her prey!

EXPENSIVE PARENTAL RESTRICTION

The guide was showing the second grade class through the Baltimore Art Museum.

"This," he said, "is a very famous painting by the French artist, Henri Matisse, who died in 1954 at the age of eighty-five. It's titled *Interior With Dog*. It was given to this museum by the Cone sisters of Baltimore. Would any of you care to guess what the value of this painting is?" Then, after a pause, "It's said to be worth twenty million dollars."

"Tell me," he continued, "What would you do with this painting if I were to give it to you?"

"I'd hang it in my room and be sure to keep the door locked," one little boy replied.

The children giggled, and then a little girl said, "That's too selfish. It should be hung in the living room so the whole family and guests could enjoy it."

"Anybody else?" the guide asked, seeking more comments.

"If you gave it to me," another little girl said, "I'd have to bring it back."

"Why – why would you do that?" the guide asked.

"Because my mother won't let me accept anything from a stranger!"

EXTENDED RITES

It went on, literally, for years.

Every Sunday the entire family would go to Mass in the morning; Mother, Father, and sons, Jim and Tom, three years apart. After church they went to Grandmother's house for Sunday dinner which consisted, always, of hot dogs, coleslaw, pork and beans, home-made bread and Jell-O with whipped cream. The routine began when the boys were infants.

After dinner they would stay the afternoon and in the evening watch the Ed Sullivan show.

Always.

Then they would return home.

The routine was the same. The food was the same.

Years went by.

Jim and Tom reached their teens and one day, Tom said to his mother, "Mom, you know that thing we did every Sunday, that going over to Grandma's house, the food she served, that watching Ed Sullivan in the evening, all that time I thought that was all a part of the Catholic religion!"

EXTRA BONUS

Five-year-old Kellie was sassing her grandmother. It went on for a few minutes, and Grandfather grabbed the child by the arm, whirled her around and said, "You listen, young lady. That's my wife you're talking to, and I want that sassing stopped right this minute!"

By the next day the incident was forgotten. In the morning the child visited a friend who had a swing set, and when she returned home she excitedly propositioned Grandma, "Grandma, will you get me a swing set?"

"I don't have any money to buy you such an expensive plaything. You'll have to work and earn your own money for that."

Kellie departed and went down to the barn where Grandpa was getting ready to take the horses to the pasture.

"Grandpa," she said, "I want to get a swing set. Will you pay me to take care of the animals? I'll feed the chickens and the pigs. I'll feed the rabbits and clean out their cages. Of course, you'll have to help me with the horses, but I'll milk the cow, feed the dogs and cats and I'll gather the eggs."

Busy with the horses, Grandpa did not respond immediately so Kellie evidently thought she must sweeten the offer.

"And I'll even be good to your wife!"

EXTREME CAUTION

Brian, age two-and-a-half, was shopping with his mother. As they were going down the aisles, Brian would spot someone and say to his mother, "Mom, who's that?"

If she knew, she would tell him, then the boy would ask, "Well do we like him (or her), Mom?"

"Yes, we like him," his mother would answer.

This was repeated with every person the boy spied, always with the same question, "Do we like him, Mom?" and Mother always patiently answering.

As they neared the checkout counter, the boy asked. "Mom, can we buy this little box of raisins?"

"Yes, I guess so."

"Can I open them now?"

Mom glanced at the checkout girl who nodded her consent. "Sure, it'll be all right." Brian opened the box and started to nibble.

As they checked out, next in line behind them was a distinguished looking, elderly gentleman.

Brian offered the box to the man, "You want some raisins, Mister?"

The man smiled appreciatively, then, seemingly to please the lad, said, "Why, yes, young man, I like raisins." He held out his hand to receive the snack.

Brian's face grew serious. He withdrew his raisins and turned to his mother:

"Hey, Mom," he said, "do we like this man?"

FAMILY LOYALTY

George sold newspapers on the corner of 58th and Chester Avenue.

He was at his station one evening about five-thirty. His sister came by stating that she was going to the nearby store for her mother.

When she came out of the store, George said, "Marie, would you take my place here for a minute or two while I run home to the bathroom. I'll take your sack on home to Mom." Home was only a hundred yards away, and Marie consented.

While George was gone, a trolley stopped at the corner and an elderly, well dressed lady got off. She walked over to Marie and bought a paper.

"My goodness, child," the lady said, "aren't you cold with no gloves or mittens?"

"Well, yeah, I guess so, a little bit." Marie hadn't really thought about it; she had been outside only a very short while.

"Here," said the lady, "you take this dollar and you buy yourself some gloves."

Marie took the bill, thanked the lady, and the lady turned to leave.

Then Marie shared one final thought with her benefactor, "I also have a little brother!"

FAMILY PAR EXCELLENCE

Andrea was five years old. Her daddy owned and operated the Brenny Dahl Block Company which dealt in ready-mix concrete and related products, and she often went out to job sites with him. She came to know the concrete business unusually well for a child of such tender years.

One hot summer day, the city was putting in new curbs and gutters in the street where they lived, and Andrea was standing on the sidewalk taking it all in.

When the work progressed to the spot exactly in front of her home, she asked the workmen, "Where are you getting your mud?"

After recovering from the shock of this little tyke's using the industry jargon, one of the men replied. "We're getting it from Arrowhead Concrete Company."

"Well, I'll tell you one thing," Andrea declared vehemently, "If you get thirsty, you better not dare come to our house and ask for a drink of water!"

FAMILY TOGETHERNESS

The Schultzes were touring the western states and had taken a back road in Wyoming. Coming over the crest of a hill they encountered a sheepherder leading a large flock across the highway. They stopped to enjoy the sight, heightened by the early summer greenness of the meadow, back dropped by beautiful, snowcapped mountains.

The sheep huddled tightly together even as they moved and the only sounds were the light rumble of the little beating hooves accompanied by the incessant "bah—ah—ah, bah—ah—ah, bah—ah—ah!"

"Gee, just look, Mommy," cried three-year-old Heidi, "there's mama ones, papa ones, and little kids ones!"

FAVORITE BOOK

Eddie was going with his mother to the hospital to visit Becky, his neighbor and schoolmate who had been injured in an accident. The mother suggested he take one of his books for the patient to look at while convalescing. Eddie prized his books and was reluctant to let them out of his possession.

In making the selection, he was torn. On the one hand, he wouldn't want anything to happen to his favorite book, and yet this is the one he would most like to show off. He finally decided on this, his very best book.

En route to the hospital he seemed a bit glum and tense, but once there, all went well. Becky was thrilled that he had brought her the book, and, seemingly sensing that it was his favorite, went overboard in expressing her appreciation.

Leaving the hospital, Eddie turned to his mother, "Gee, Mommy, wasn't that nice of me!"

FAVORITE SPORT

The Sunday School teacher was trying to make the new three-year-old enrollee feel at home. She could see that the child was anxious about his new experience, so she tried to question him in a casual and friendly manner.

"What do you like to do, Nathaniel?" she asked.

The boy remained silent, fidgeted a bit, and seemed totally stumped by this simple question.

"Come, Nathaniel, tell me, what do you like to do?"

The child was utterly blank. Not only could he not answer the question, it seemed he could not even speak.

"Oh, come, Nathaniel, there must be lots of things. Every boy has his favorite thing he likes to do. Come on, what's yours?"

Finally there came a new light in the boy's eyes, and the teacher sensed that an answer was forthcoming at last. Then the child smiled and said: "I like to pick my nose!"

FICKLE MOURNER

Joanna was devastated. She was sobbing and crying her heart out. When she had asked her friend, Lisa, to come out and play, Lisa had said she couldn't because she was helping her dad give Angel, their dog, a bath. All pets have to be bathed once in a while, Lisa had said.

Consequently, Joanna had given her pet, Cindy, a bath. The problem arose out of the fact that Cindy was a goldfish. She had taken her from her bowl, soaped and rubbed her well, and returned her to her abode, but now she was belly up and barely moving a fin.

The child went screaming and crying to her mother who said, "What on earth happened to Cindy? She was okay a little while ago."

"Well, Lisa said you should bathe your pets, so I did, and now I think she's dying." The child wailed on and on.

"Well, we'll just have to wait and see what happens. Maybe she'll be all right, but you mustn't be too disappointed if she dies; she isn't showing much life."

This set the child in a still worse state, crying as though it were surely the end of the world.

Hoping to console the girl, her mother said, "Well, now, Honey, don't carry on so. I'll tell you what; it's no big tragedy. We can get another goldfish."

"I don't want another goldfish; I want Cindy," the child insisted, sobbing.

That afternoon the child's Aunt Eileen stopped in to see if Joanna's mother could go shopping with her. "I can't, but if you will, you might take

Joanna with you. Maybe you can cheer her up; she's heartbroken because her goldfish might die."

Joanna's mother dressed the child for the shopping trip, but there was still whimpering as the pair got in the car.

"I'll tell you what, Joanna," her aunt said, "if Cindy dies, I'll buy you *two* goldfish. Then they can keep each other company."

Immediately the tears vanished; the sad expression was replaced with a smile.

"Wait a minute, Aunt Eileen," the child said, "let me go see if Cindy's dead yet!"

FIELD TRIP

Chuckie sat down to dinner. "Is this cow's milk?" he asked.

"Yes, of course," his mother answered.

"I don't want cow's milk, I want dairy milk," the boy stated emphatically.

"But dairy milk is cow's milk," the mother explained.

"Oh, no, it isn't," the boy insisted, "you can't fool me about that any more. From now on I'm drinking dairy milk and that's all!"

"Now, Chuckie, listen to me. Dairy milk *is* cow's milk."

"Oh, no, it isn't. Our class took a trip through the dairy yesterday and there wasn't a cow in the whole building!"

FINANCIAL CENTER

Russell had moved with his parents from Des Moines to Davenport.

Returning to Des Moines for a visit, he was telling his friends all about Davenport. "Davenport has the Palmer School of Chiropractic, Davenport has the 'Little Bit 'O Heaven.'" Davenport has this, Davenport has that.

"And you may not believe this," he said, "but Davenport has the *First National Bank!*"

FLASH BULB SUPREME

The storm had been brewing all evening. Pam had been put to bed at the usual nine o'clock, but shortly thereafter came a blinding bolt of lightning with an almost simultaneous, deafening clap of thunder.

Dad and Mom ran pell-mell up the stairs to comfort Pam and assure her all was well and there was nothing to be afraid of.

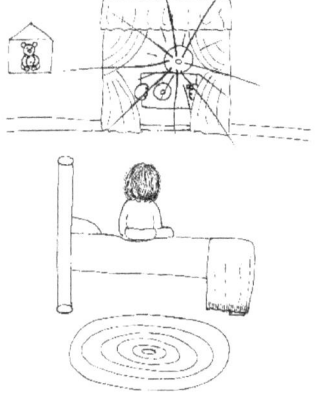

They found the child just bursting out her door as she shouted, "Mommy, Daddy, God just came to my window and took my picture!"

FLEXING MUSCLES

At the family holiday gathering, Dustin and his grandfather had to get reacquainted as they had not seen each other for two years, and the lad was now six.

"Come over here, young man," Grandfather said, "and let me feel your muscle."

The boy made a fist and bent his arm upward as the grandfather squeezed the upper arm. "Boy, what a muscle, you'll make a good football player or prize fighter."

"Now let me feel yours, Grandpa," the boy said.

Grandpa chuckled but made a fist and bent his arm for the boy to feel. Dustin grasped the upper arm. Then he moved his hand from elbow to shoulder, squeezing slightly at intervals. His face took on a puzzled expression. Then he moved his hand under the arm and felt a bit further. As though deeply perplexed and somewhat embarrassed, the child said, "Gee, Grandpa, your muscle has all melted and run down under your arm!"

FLUNKING THE FINAL EXAM

Jimmy at age five was complaining to his father that Charlie, not quite three, was all mixed up about meals. He might call breakfast lunch, dinner breakfast, etc.

"Well, okay," Dad said, "why don't you teach him. That'll be a nice little project for you. You teach him, and tonight when I come home, I'll expect him to know the difference between breakfast, lunch and dinner."

So Jimmy spent much of the day drilling his younger brother. "The meal when you first get up in the morning, that's breakfast; then in the middle of the day you have lunch; then at night, we have dinner. Now, you tell me, what is it we have when we first get up?"

"Beckfast."

"Okay, and what do we have at night?"

"Dinner."

"And what do we eat in the middle of the day?"

"Lunch."

Jimmy asked the questions over and over and in a different order; every time Charlie got it right.

That night when dad came home, Jimmy reported his success in the assignment his dad had given him.

At dinner, Dad said to Charlie, "Charlie, what is it you're eating now?"

"Rice!"

FOLLOWING ORDERS

My son, Bob, when in his forties, had three generation guests at his summer cabin: his friend Jerry Carlson, the latter's father and also Jerry's son, Jeremy, age about three years.

In the evening they decided to go out in the boat and catch some fish for breakfast. Although Jeremy was too young for serious fishing, Bob wanted to keep him from being bored by drawing him into the action, insofar as possible, so when Bob got a fish on his line, he said excitedly, "Jeremy, get the net!"

The child grabbed the landing net and took up a position near Bob. He held up the net and intently watched the water where the line was being reeled in. The fish came into view. It was a nice one, would weigh three pounds, maybe more.

"Jeremy," Bob said, "put the net in the water." The boy lowered the net a bit, but it was still some inches from the water.

"Jeremy, put the net in the water," Bob repeated. The lad looked at Bob; there was a very peculiar look on the child's face—as though he was puzzled and perhaps embarrassed.

The fish was fighting and flopping more furiously now. "Jeremy, put the net in the water," Bob ordered emphatically.

The next day Bob did three things:

    Cooked bacon and eggs for his guests' breakfast.

    Bought a new landing net.

    Resolved that he would learn to be more explicit when giving instructions.

You see, when Bob had said to the lad for the third time. "Jeremy, put the net in the water," Jeremy did exactly that—and it sank to the bottom!

FOUR-LETTER WORDS

The dairy bill had been fouled up three months in a row, and the housewife again nailed the milkman who had tried each time to straighten out the matter. Phoning back to his office, his side of the conversation went something like this: "Damn it all, why the hell can't you keep this account straight? This is the third month now, and these people jump me about it, and I don't blame them, but I just ain't going to take the rap for it anymore. Either you get it corrected or I'm going to the boss about it!"

He banged down the receiver. Before he left, all was smoothed out between the deliveryman and the customer, but after he was gone, little Eva who had taken it all in said, "Mommy, that man said a bad word."

The mother was curious as to what had triggered her daughter's remark. "Why, dear," she asked, "what did he say?"

"You heard, Mommy, you know very well what he said," was the shy reply.

"I'm not sure I do, dear. Tell me, what was it he said?"

"You know, Mommy, you know very well. That man said 'ain't!'"

FRANKNESS IN CHURCH

Mr. Crawford had played the piano in the little country church for seven years. One Sunday he was playing something that he knew well; it had become so routine that he was really off somewhere in dreamland.

Suddenly he felt a slight tug on his sleeve near the elbow. Normally he would have continued to play while turning to see who wanted his attention, but now, in his reverie, he was so startled that he abruptly stopped playing.

The congregation had seen what was happening, and most members were smiling in amusement.

Mr. Crawford turned and looked up, then down, into the face of a two-year-old boy. The child had toddled off, unseen, from the nursery.

The slight titter that had arisen as the boy approached the pianist subsided, and the church was silent.

"Hey, Mister," said the tot, "your moosic is getting on my nurse!"

FRUIT OF PROPER UPBRINGING

Teasing is not supposed to justify physical violence, but there is, in some of us, a breaking point. There definitely was in five-year-old Edward. His friend Randy teased him and kept pouring it on till he finally pushed Edward over the edge, whereupon the latter picked up a rock and hurled it with unfortunate accuracy.

The stone caught Randy in the back of the head and he went down. Unsteadily, he rose and ran home, crying.

Soon Randy's mother phoned Edward's mother, and Edward was taken by the ear and led over to confront the injured neighbors.

Although it appeared that Randy had his faculties, he was still sobbing, and an ugly bump had risen on his head at the point of impact.

Edward's mother uttered her own apology to Randy and his mother, then turned to her own son, "Edward, tell Randy you're sorry," she said.

Edward stood stubbornly silent.

"Edward, tell Randy you're sorry," his mother repeated.

Still no word from Edward.

"Edward Johnston, you tell Randy you're sorry!"

Still silence.

"Edward Johnston, do you hear me?"

"Yes, Mom."

"Then why won't you tell Randy you're sorry?"

"Because you've told me I always have to tell the truth, and *I'm not sorry!*"

FULL SCHEDULE

Carole, eight, was the active type while her sister Cathie was more of a homebody.

They were spending a month at the seashore with their parents.

When they had been on their vacation a couple of weeks, Grandma called. After talking with the children's parents, she asked to talk to the children. Cathie talked first, and toward the end of their conversation, the child said, "Gee, I miss you, Grandma."

"Well, I miss you too, dear. Now let me talk to Carole."

"Hello Grandma," Carole said, taking the phone.

"Hi, Honey, do you miss your grandma too?"

"No, I haven't got around to it yet!"

FULLY PROTECTED

Because Milton was only six, Mama wasn't fully reconciled to his learning to water ski, but Dad and Milton's older brother and sister were gung ho to teach him.

Thus, Mama's was a minority vote, and she showed her concern as Milton donned the life preserver, slipped off the dock into the water and his sister helped him harness his feet onto the skis. Dad started the motor and pulled slowly away from the dock as Milton's older brother fed out the tow rope from the boat's stern.

Milton glanced back at his mother sitting on the dock. Sensing her anxiety, the boy said:

"Cute kids don't get hurt, Mom!"

GARGANTUAN THIRST

It was hot and humid, and the flies were biting. Dad had been swiping with his hand at the pests but wasn't having much success. Suddenly, with a quick sweep of the hand, he captured one. He picked it out of his fist with the thumb and forefinger of his left hand and held it by the wing. Encouraged by his victory over the pest and now determined to rid the room of the nuisance, he said to his two-year-old daughter, "Erica, go get me the fly swatter."

The child left the room and soon returned. She was carrying a glass of water and offered it to her dad.

"What's that; what's that for?" her father asked.

"It's the fly's water!"

GETTING EVEN

Grandma was to be entertained for Mother's Day dinner by her two sons, their wives and four small grandchildren. Arriving at the chosen restaurant, it was discovered that a previous night's storm had disrupted power, and the eatery had found it necessary to close.

Selection of another place then became a matter for discussion. Rachael, at five years old, was quick with her suggestion—McDonald's. Other suggestions were made with no one paying any attention to Rachael's request. The more she was ignored, the louder became her plea to go to her favorite hamburger emporium till finally her parents shushed her.

Several suggestions were made, and it was necessary to consider the factor of restaurants having record crowds due to the special occasion. Finally, an agreement was reached, and it was, of course, over Rachael's protests. Grandma seemed to grasp the child's disappointment, gave her a warm little squeeze and whispered, "I like McDonald's, too."

The group drove to the newly selected restaurant, and it happened that Grandma and Rachael were in different cars. When they arrived, Rachel sidled up to the elder and whispered, "Grandma, I've been thinking, let's you and I just not eat!"

GIVE ME TIME

When Dicky was only four he gave his mother as succinct an answer as might be forthcoming from the most articulate adult.

She had discovered the crayon drawings on newly decorated walls and was aghast.

"Why on earth did you do that?" she cried.

The swiftness, too, of the reply helped set it apart as a classic: "'Cause I'm just a little kid and I don't have very much good sense yet!"

GOOD QUESTION

Miscellaneous relatives were lolling on the dock, passing time on a lazy afternoon. There was a bit of banter about the various relationships. In the course of this conversation, there was some explaining to the children as to which person was related to whom and in what way.

Brian's father, Dan, had divorced his first wife and was currently married to Charlotte, who was now Brian's stepmother. Dan pointed to his father-in-law saying, "Charlotte is his kid."

Charlotte being thirty-five, Brian promptly responded, "She's no kid, she's a grown-up."

"Nevertheless, she's still my kid," interjected the grandfather, "always was and always will be."

"Sure, Brian," said Dan, "you're my kid and you always will be my kid, even when you're forty."

Brian pondered a moment, then seemed to accept the reality and asked, "Will you still yell at me then?"

GOURMET

The teacher was explaining about the various parts of the mouth and their functions. Amplifying on the description and function of the taste buds, she went on to say that there were four fundamental flavors which excited the gustatory nerves.

"These are salt, sweet, sour, and—," but at this juncture, her memory failed and she could not call to mind the fourth: bitter.

She paused, puzzled, then stated again: "salt, sweet, sour…and…can anyone tell me what the fourth taste is?"

A hand went up in the back of the room, and when the teacher nodded, the reply shot back, "Just right!"

GRANDPA, JACK-OF-ALL-TRADES

As an adult, Steve now tells this story on himself. At exactly what age this occurred, he does not remember.

Grandpa had come for a visit. It was approaching dinnertime, and Steve had washed his hands as he was taught to do before each meal.

Dinner was delayed a bit and suddenly Steve said to Grandpa, "Grandpa, would you come and do something for me?"

"Sure, Son, what is it?"

Steve went to the bathroom, Grandfather following. The boy stood at the stool and unzipped his trousers.

"Grandpa," he said, "I have to go, would you take it out of my pants for me?"

"Heaven's sakes, boy, why?"

"'Cause I've already washed my hands for dinner, and I don't want to have to wash 'em again!"

GRAPHIC LABELING

The neighborhood children were playing when suddenly a new puppy, not seen in the area before, joined the group.

The newcomer was frisking about from child to child getting acquainted when one of them asked, "Is it a boy or a girl puppy?" One of the older boys grabbed the dog, and,] as the others gathered around, turned it over and announced, "It's a boy puppy."

Three-year-old Jennifer pushed her way through the group, gazed at the overturned animal and asked excitedly, "Where does it say that? Where does it say that?"

GRIEVOUS OVERSIGHT

Four-year-old Adam and his mother were exceedingly close, lots of snuggling, lots of hugging and kissing and frequent assertions as to the depth of mother love.

Mother's sister was getting married and Mom was helping with, among other things, the wedding invitations.

"Whatcha doin', Mom?" Adam wanted to know.

"Well, I'm helping your Aunt Doris with her wedding invitations."

"What does that mean?"

"Well, she's getting married next month. She's going to have a wedding."

"What's a wedding?"

"A wedding is a sort of celebration. When a man and woman decide they love each other so much that they want to spend all the rest of their lives together, they get married, and they have this celebration that's called a wedding. They invite their loved ones, relatives and friends to come and hear them declare that they love each other and are going to live together like, well, like Daddy and me. "

"So what are those things you're writing?"

"These are invitations; they'll be mailed to all the relatives and friends inviting them to come to the wedding."

This ended the questions for a while, but Adam appeared to grow pensive. He went and watched a bit of TV but soon he turned off the set and came back.

"Mom," he asked, "if you love me so much, how come you didn't invite me to your wedding?"

HALF A LOAF IS BETTER THAN NONE

Gary and Amelia were going steady – well, almost – as steady, that is, as nine-year-olds usually get.

The relationship was pleasantly accepted by Gary's parents, as Amelia, was, indeed, a nice and personable lass.

Came July, vacation time, and Gary and his family went to the seashore for a month.

Enter now into the scene, Rita, a cute little seven-year-old. Gary observed her frolicking in the surf, decided to move in, and soon was building her an elaborate castle in the sand.

At the end of three days of rather constant companionship, Gary said to his father, "Dad, how do you like Rita?"

"Oh, I like her fine, but I don't really think she has as much personality as Amelia has!"

"Yeah, I know, Dad, that's probably true, but I can lower my standards a little while I'm on vacation!"

HAND ME DOWN

Megan's aunt had come to visit, and there was much conversation that day between Megan's mother and her sister (the aunt) about family antiques. They examined and talked about those things around the house that were prized because of their sentimental value, the attachments which stemmed from their having come down from the sisters' parents and grandparents.

That night, when tucking Megan in, the child's mother bent down and gave the child a loving kiss. Playfully, the child clung to her mother as they further exchanged kisses.

Then the mother squeezed the child and gave her a resounding smack, held the child away, then drew her back again saying, "I guess maybe I'll take that one back, that was such a wonderful kiss, I guess I want it back!"

"Yeah, I know," Megan responded, "because that's one you got from your mother!"

HE SEES YOU WHEN YOU'RE SLEEPING, HE KNOWS WHEN YOU'RE AWAKE

When Chuckie climbed up onto Santa's lap, what he didn't know was that he was really on the lap of a neighbor who was a good friend of his parents and knew many of the family "secrets."

A few weeks earlier, Chuckie had kicked his little brother in the back creating an uproar which included a trip to the hospital. Fortunately, the injury was not serious, but the fallout of the incident did occasionally surface in the form of sibling rancor during family give-and-take.

The incident was totally out of Chuckie's thoughts when he reported his year's behavior to the bright-eyed, bewhiskered St. Nick. His recital was well thought out and rehearsed; it closely followed the theme of his favorite Christmas song, "Santa Claus Is Comin' To Town."

He began, "I watched out; I didn't cry; I didn't pout; I haven't been naughty; I've been nice; I haven't been bad; I've been good; I've been good for goodness' sake, and—and—and—"

At this point, Santa could not resist finishing the sentence, "and I kicked my little brother in the back!"

Chuckie was devastated! He didn't cry, but he dropped off of Santa's lap like a zombie.

It was an hour or more after the party before Chuckie spoke, and then it was with a contrite attitude that he said to his parents, "Boy, that Santa Claus really *does* find out if you've been naughty or nice!"

HIDDEN GOLD

For several days, Mom had noticed a peculiar odor whenever she went into Carla's room. At first she gave the matter only slight thought, but the problem failed to go away.

Finally she began looking in earnest and eventually was led to a bureau drawer. As she opened it, the odor doubled – well – maybe tripled!

A purse seemed suspect and when she opened it, the stench leaped out at her. Inside she discovered a rotten goldfish. She went to the family aquarium to find that Chubby, Carla's favorite and the prettiest and most prized of the goldfish, was missing.

When Carla returned from school, Mom confronted the child with the evidence. "Carla," she demanded, "what on earth ever possessed you to put this fish in your purse?"

The child began to cry, "W—ww—well, the—th—there was this m—m—man on TV who—who said you should w—w—walk your dog every day, so – so I thought I ought to walk Chubby, so I p—p—put him in my purse and took him for – for a walk and then I – I – I guess I forgot about it!"

HIGHER MATH

Timmy broke out in a terrible rash two days after having had a shot. His mother rushed him back to the doctor who took his temperature and pulse and looked him over carefully.

"Timmy," he said thoughtfully, "that shot might have caused an allergic reaction, but nothing as severe as this." Then, turning toward Tim's mother, "Anything new in your house—plants, animals, any different soap or chemicals?"

"No, nothing."

"Timmy, have you been going any different places, handling anything different outside?" the doctor asked.

"No."

"Have you been handling anything different at school?"

"Yeah, division!"

HOME IMPROVEMENT

After an absence during which they had rented out their house, the Johnstons, upon moving back in, had the entire house redecorated inside and out.

The front door and entryway were done in sparkling white—white, that is, until Mrs. Johnston discovered that three-year-old Edward had found a can of paint and was "redoing" the outside of the door in flaming orange!

"Edward," she screamed, "where on earth did you get that horrid paint? You've ruined that door!"

Edward had seen his mother enraged before and he responded in a manner he hoped would prevent mayhem. He did not rise from his squatting position, and, with paint brush still in hand, merely said in a quiet, steady voice, slowly nodding his head affirmatively, "You'll like it better, Mom, when it's dry!"

HORTICULTURAL SLIP UP

Freddie knew what a widow was. That was a woman whose husband had died, and that was sad. More sad now was the fact that Mrs. Davis had broken her ankle and could not attend to any of the chores around the acreage.

He knew that many of the neighbors were pitching in to help out in the emergency, and one day his mother took him with her when she went to Mrs. Davis's home to assist with some housework.

Freddie was fond of Mrs. Davis and had the urge to help too and after spending some time in the garden he brought Mrs. Davis a bowl saying, "Look, I picked your radishes for you."

The lady had no particular appetite for radishes at the moment but wished to show that she appreciated the boy's desire to help. "Oh, thank you, Freddie, how nice—" but then she stopped short, a bit shocked, having noticed that he was holding a bowl of peony buds!

ILLEGAL ACT

Siri, age four, and Jacob, age seven, were admiring the glitter decorations on their mother's sweatshirt.

"Thanks," Mom said, "I did that lettering myself."

Then Jacob looked at his mother. "It's pretty, Mom, but you know you can be arrested for doing it and have to pay a fine."

"That's right, Mom," Siri chimed in. "You can be arrested, and you might even go to jail."

"What in the world are you two talking about?" their mother asked.

"It's true, Mom," Jacob responded. "You see the signs all over: *One hundred Dollar Fine for Littering!*"

ILLITERACY IN ACTION

Sean stood in awe whenever someone looked at a piece of paper, ran his eyes across those odd markings and recited a story. "Reading" was a concept beyond his comprehension when he was two. Eventually he learned that the story was contained in those strange markings that were called letters. Letters made up words, and just by looking at a group of letters one could know the word and put all the words together and make a story.

What a fascinating world!

Next he learned that Mother and Father and even his older sister could put the letters on a piece of paper to create words— it was called writing.

"I want to learn how to read and write, Mommy," he said.

"You'll learn that when you go to school," his mother replied.

"Well, when can I go to school?"

"When you're older. You start school when you're five."

But the child's avid interest in learning led his parents to locate a suitable pre-school, and in mid-summer they told him, "Sean, we've arranged for you to go to pre-school. You'll be starting early in September."

The child's eyes grew wide with delight!

"I can learn to read and write?" he asked excitedly.

"Yes, you can learn to read and write and do numbers and lots of other things."

Sean spread the news far and wide. "I'm going to go to school. I'm going to learn to read and write." His friends and sometimes pure strangers were let in on the news.

August seemed an eternity, and finally came the Labor Day weekend.

To his questions came the answer, "Yes, Honey, next Tuesday; you'll begin next Tuesday morning."

Saturday dragged by. Sunday and Monday were still another eternity. There was little or no sleep Monday night, but nevertheless the child seemed fresh and alive Tuesday morning.

"Now, Honey, this first half year, you'll only be going half days. Today, I'll pick you up at noon."

"Okay, g'bye, Mommy, g'bye."

When his mother picked him up at noon, the smiles had vanished. Glumly the child took his mother's hand, and they walked to the parking lot. Once seated in the car, Sean began to cry.

"Honey, Honey, what's wrong, what happened?"

Between sobs came the sad reply, "They didn't teach me how to read and write!"

IMPOVERISHED TEACHER

A few weeks after Brian had entered kindergarten, he was walking and suddenly saw his teacher in a side yard. She was leaning over some sort of a stand that was smoking.

He walked toward her and said "Hi, Mrs. Jackson, is this where you live?"

"Yes, what brings you by here?"

"Oh, I live just over there," Brian said, pointing. I'm going to the store for my mom. What's that you're doing?"

"I'm barbequing."

"What's that mean?"

"I'm cooking; I'm cooking dinner."

Brian thought for a moment, his expression reflecting puzzlement, then sadness. "Gee, that's too bad, Mrs. Jackson," he said, "I wish you had a nice kitchen stove like my mom's!"

IMPROPER EQUIPMENT

Kim's father was a fireman. Vaguely, at three years old, she knew what this meant. Occasionally fire trucks came clanging by and she knew that somewhere a house or some building was burning and that it was the job of the men on the truck to go put the fire out; she, of course, had heard her daddy talking about it.

However, she had never seen where her daddy worked and curiosity now prompted her to want to visit his place of employment, so on a Saturday, Dad agreed to take the family across town to the fire station.

Kim pointed to a truck. "What truck is that?" she asked.

"That's a water truck," her dad responded.

"And what truck is that?" she asked pointing to another.

"That's a water truck, too," came the reply.

"Well, where's the fire truck?"

IMPROVED ENGINEERING

Three-and-a-half-year-old Pace was watching his neighbor install a swimming pool. It was a hot and humid day, and the neighbor was dirty and sweating under the strain of hard, physical labor.

"Gee, Mr. Fisher, isn't that awfully hard work?" the child asked.

"Yes it is, Pace, it's very hard work."

"I wouldn't do it that way if I was doing it," the child said.

In spite of his mood, Mr. Fisher managed a smile, "Just how would you do it, Pace?" he asked.

"I'd go to the store and buy a round rubber pool, put it on the ground and fill it with water!"

INADEQUATE EQUIPMENT

Grandma was fussing at Kelly. "Young lady," she said, "what on earth is the matter with you today? I told you to take that trash out— you haven't done it. I told you to hang up your things—you haven't done it. Told you to put your trike away—you haven't done it. What on earth has gotten into you anyway?"

"Well, gee, Grandma, I had an awful day in school, just an awful day," the child replied.

"Well, what was so bad about today? Usually you like school; what happened today?"

"Oh, we were doing arithmetic, and I just had a terrible time with it."

"But you've done real well with arithmetic before."

"I know, but today we were doing take a-ways. I couldn't do 'em at all."

"But you did take a-ways just last week. You told me you liked them; you thought they were fun."

"Yeah, I know, but today the teacher started doing bigger ones, and I couldn't do 'em 'cause I only have ten fingers!"

INNOCENT BY ASSOCIATION

Fifty years ago, punishment for misbehavior in school was on a far different plane from what it is today.

The principal was attempting to establish respectable-looking grounds and one section of the schoolyard was declared to be off limits. Nevertheless, with a macho attitude, a group of five boys decided to do some testing of this new rule. They were observed, and taken to the principal's office.

An appropriate lecture was given the group and then the principal asked a boy his name. He then took his pencil and on a sheet of paper evidently wrote down the name, told the boy to come forward, asked him to bend over, and gave him a resounding whack with a paddle which he kept in his office for just such disciplinary purposes. Then a second boy was called, and the routine was repeated, followed by a third boy. The fourth boy was called, and when he was asked his name, he responded, "Roy Christensen."

"Well now, boys," the principal said, "I have a bad arm, and it's difficult for me to use this paddle. I want you to go on to your classes and in the future observe the school rules."

It is now a half century later, and Christensen reflects, "It'll always be my opinion that when the principal heard my name, he suddenly remembered that there was a Christensen, my father, on the school board!"

INSTANT GENEROSITY

Mike at age five was very possessive of his material things and his mother was trying to teach him to share.

"Mike," she said, "you must learn to share. When you have an apple, you should give your sister half. I'm not saying you must; if you have an apple, it's yours and no one else has a right to it, but it's a nice thing to learn to share."

The next day, a report came from school that Mike had misbehaved. This not being the first time, his father decided the youngster needed something more memorable than a scolding, so he turned the lad over his knee.

Whack! Whack!

"Daddy, Daddy, stop," the boy protested. "I want to give half of this to my sister!"

INSTANT PROMOTION

Waldo had just received his wings and was now a second lieutenant. He was in full uniform when he landed at the airport to visit his brother, Jim.

Jim Jr. viewed his uncle with awe, seeming almost hypnotized by the dazzle of the uniform.

At home, the family visited for a while and then Waldo said he'd like to go to his room and change his clothes.

"Wait, Uncle Waldo, wait," the younger Jim cried excitedly, "I'll be right back; I'll just be a minute!" The lad raced out of the house. In four or five minutes he returned, out of breath, and with him was a friend.

"Uncle Waldo," he said, "This is my friend, Tony. Tony, this is my uncle, Waldo. He's a policeman!"

INTENSIVE CARE

In route home from the basketball game where eight-year-old Charlie had distinguished himself by actually shooting a basket, there was exciting talk. "I'm gonna play basketball when I get to high school and when I get to college, too."

Brother Kelly, a year and a half younger, was not about to be overshadowed. "When I get to high school and college, I'm gonna play football, that's what I'm gonna do!"

"Well, now, young man," his mother interposed, "you'd better think twice about that. Football is a very rough game, and you can get hurt pretty badly."

"Yeah, I know, Mom, but they take care of stuff like that. They have Band-Aids!"

INTERESTING CONTEST, BUT WHO WON?

At three and a half years of age, Mark could be very stubborn.

The family was in the car and ready to leave for an outing at the lake. It was a hot day, and Dad thought it would be nice if they each had a popsicle. He unfastened his seat belt, turned off the engine and went back into the house and got popsicles for the two boys, his wife and himself.

"I don't want this kind," Mark said.

Patiently, Dad went back in the house and got him a different flavor.

"I don't want this kind either."

"I'll go," Mom said, "I know what he wants."

Mom brought back an Eskimo Pie. Mark took it eagerly but said nothing.

"What do you say to your mother?" Dad asked the boy.

Silence.

"Mark, what do you say to your mother?"

Nothing.

"Mark, I want you to thank your mother." Dad's voice was now stern and insistent.

Mark simply kept licking and nibbling on the Eskimo Pie.

Stuart, two years older than Mark, was growing impatient. "Come on Mark, just say it; ya don't have to mean it."

"Thanks, Mom."

"You're welcome, Son," Mom said.

Dad started the car and slipped it into gear.

INVOLUNTARY RETIREE

Grandpa had come to visit and in the third week, Freddie, age six, asked his mother, "How long is Grandpa going to stay? Doesn't he have to get back to work?"

"No, Grandpa doesn't work, he's retired," the boy's mother replied.

"Could he come to school and visit some day?"

"Certainly, I think he'd enjoy that. I think that would be nice."

Freddie asked his teacher about his grandfather visiting school, and she replied, "Oh, yes, we'd love to have him come. Bring him anytime you like."

The next day Grandpa came with Freddie, and as soon as the bell rang, the teacher said, "Now, Freddie, would you like to introduce your grandfather and tell us where he's from and what he does."

"This is my grandfather," Freddie announced as the elder rose to his feet. "His name is Mr. Walker and he lives in Omaha."

"It's nice to have you, Mr. Walker," the teacher said nodding. "Now, Freddie, what kind of work does Mr. Walker do?"

"Oh, he doesn't work. He's retarded!"

JEFF'S CREDIBILITY GAP

Ashley, three, was telling his cousin, Jeff, who was eight, all about what Santa Claus had brought him for Christmas.

"But there isn't any Santa Claus. It's not true," Jeff said. "Your parents give you all that stuff."

It was obvious that Ashley was shaken by the news but he did not know whether Jeff was teasing or telling the truth.

Now that Christmas was approaching again, and there were all the many indications of the coming holidays, Ashley's thoughts were back again on the question.

"But Jeff told me there isn't any Santa Claus. You keep talking about him. Is there or isn't there?" he asked his father.

"Well, we think there is. Of course nobody ever really sees him. The Santa Clauses that you see in the stores and on the street corners are really only people dressed up to look like what we all think Santa Claus looks like. This is done to spread the spirit of giving and get us in the joyful mood for Christmas. You'll have to decide for yourself whether Santa Claus is real."

Time as it always will, had dulled the image and impact of Christmases past, so as Ashley was tucked in on Christmas Eve, it was obvious that he was still uncertain.

"But anyhow, I have been a good boy, haven't I? Well, mostly anyway?" he asked.

"Yes, you have, mostly you have, and we both love you very much. Now you get a good night's sleep, and in the morning you can find out whether or not you think there's a Santa Claus."

When the child had departed the living room that night, there was a tree with lights, but when he descended the stairs the next morning, he walked into a dazzling fairyland. Tinsel had been added to the tree, which sparkled as it caught the sunlight from a nearby window. Colorful gifts and toys were hanging on the tree and spread out over much of the living room floor.

Ashley stood on the bottom step, viewing the spectacle, transfixed, his eyes wide, his face beaming.

"Boy, oh, boy," he said, "that darn Jeff sure is some kind of a nut!"

JIMMY HAS A POINT THERE

Jimmy had been put to bed, but he soon emerged from his room. "Did I put my trike away?" he asked.

Suspecting this to be just an excuse for getting out of bed, his father snapped, "Yes, you did. I told you to put it away and you did. Now you trot yourself right back to bed."

Soon again the child was up and came into the living room. "Is it next year I'll be going to school?" he asked.

"Yes, it is next year, but now you get back in that bed and not another peep out of you."

"How long is a year?"

"A year is a long time." Father got up and took the boy by the shoulders. "Now you listen, young man. You get back in that bed, and don't you dare come out here again unless it's about something important and I mean *important*!"

The parents thought this surely would be the end of the problem, but in four or five minutes, the lad emerged again.

"What if the house catches on fire?" he asked.

His father jumped up, gave the child a swat on the bottom and roughly ushered him back to bed. Jimmy started to cry and after a minute or two his mother could not resist trying her hand at quieting him.

Between sobs, the child said to her, "I just thought and thought and thought and I thought it would surely be important if our house catches on fire!"

JIMMY'S DRUTHERS

Jimmy received a 'B' on his composition, which is here reproduced verbatim:

"I am a camel. I don't like being a camel. It is hot in the desert and sometimes I get thirsty in the hot sun. When I cross the desert my feet sink down in the sand. Sometimes the sand is too hot for my feet. When we get across the desert my master does not have anything to do so we start back and I usually get too tired to go further so we rest for a while. Then I get hot again. I'd rather be a Polar Bear."

KEVIN'S CONQUEST

Part I

"What am I supposed to call him?" Brian asked referring to his stepmother's father. "Am I supposed to call him 'Bob' or what?"

"Well, now, it really isn't appropriate for a child to call an adult by his first name," Brian's aunt interjected. "How about calling him Grandpa?"

"I'm not going to call him Grandpa! He's not my grandpa!"

"Well, why don't you ask him what you should call him? You don't need to be afraid to talk to him about it. Ask him."

Enter into the conversation, Brian's seven-year-old younger brother, Kevin. "I'll ask him. I'm not afraid to talk to him. I'm not afraid to talk to anyone…" (pause) "There's only one person I'm afraid to talk to."

"Yes? And who's that?" the boys' father asked.

"Girls!"

Part II

Further pursuing this line of talk, Kevin said, "I get really embarrassed when I talk to girls."

"There was this one girl I like on the school bus." After a pause…"I kissed her."

"You did?" his father asked, rather amazed.

"Yup."

"Where was this?"

"On the bus."

"What did she do?"

"Nothing."

"What did she say?"

"Nothing."

"You mean she didn't say anything?"

"Nope."

"How come?"

"She was asleep!"

LACK OF SPECIFICITY

Eight-year-old Brandon was being punished. He was confined to his room for the evening for teasing his little sister, setting her off on a crying jag.

"And if you don't learn how to treat your sister, you'll get some real punishment," his mother threatened.

"Yeah, sure, you've always got plenty of punishments, but you never have any rewards—never any rewards when I do something good."

"You're *supposed* to be good. Being good doesn't earn rewards. Doing something extra special is what should bring a reward."

"Something extra special like what?"

"Well, I'll tell you what would be extra special in your case. I'd like to see a paper from school with an 'A' on it. That would be extra special. You haven't brought me a paper with a good grade since way last semester."

"So... if I bring you a paper with an 'A' on it, what'll be the reward?"

"Anytime you bring me a school paper with an 'A' on it, you can have money for the next Saturday's movie. In fact, you can even have money to take a friend."

The very next day after Brandon got home from school, he brought his mother an English paper with an 'A.' Furthermore, the teacher had written on the paper, "Very well done."

Yes, it was Brandon's handwriting, his work, no doubt about it. Brandon's mother was delighted. "It just goes to show you that you can do it when you want to. That's wonderful. Here's your dollar for the movie. You can take Joey or Tom, whomever you want."

A half-hour or so passed, then:

"*Brandon!*"

"Yes, Mom."

"Brandon, you come here, and you come here this instant."

Brandon came, but Brandon was grinning.

"What Mom?"

"Don't you 'what mom' me; you know very well 'what.' This paper is the one you wrote way last April. Now you tell me 'what!'"

"But, mom, you only said to bring you a school paper with an 'A.' You didn't say anything about when it had to be dated!"

LAST MINUTE DILEMMA

David was in first grade and was learning how to print. Rachael, his older sister, was helping him write his letter to Santa Claus. After the letter was finished and mailed, it appeared that the load was off his mind. That was out of the way and he was all set for Christmas.

A few days later in school the teacher wrote something on the blackboard in which all the letters of a word were connected. She stated that this was the way most adults wrote and that as soon as the class had mastered printing, they would be learning to write by this method.

There was the usual excitement on Christmas Eve and all seemed well when the children were put to bed. However, some minutes later David was heard crying. His mother went to his room and asked. "What's the matter, Sweetie, what's wrong?"

"Well, I just was thinking: I wrote my letter to Santa in printing. What will happen if he writes in cursive?"

LEARNING BY DOING

Ann and her brother, John, were talking. The gist of the conversation was that inasmuch as they were getting older, they should start learning to do the things adults do. They were getting older, truly, every day. In fact, Ann was six and John was four.

Their mother was away but Dad was working in the den. They went to him and Ann said, "Daddy, we've decided we want to learn to smoke."

After recovering from shock, Dad thought, "Maybe not a bad idea. Their first experience with the weed can be right here under my eye, and I can see that they get enough to really appreciate it!"

He got three of his strongest cigars and invited the children to sit with him on the living room floor and they all lit up.

John took a puff, coughed, looked a bit bewildered, then simply sat holding the cigar.

"Come on, Son, you have to keep puffing to really learn how to smoke like a man."

The boy took two more puffs, coughed, rested then took a few more. He sat as though numb for a few seconds, then decided he'd like to lie down. He did—right there on the floor. When Dad urged him to sit up and continue the smoking lesson, he said, "Oh, gee Dad, I'm not sure I want to learn!"

Meanwhile Ann was performing similarly except that she seemed a bit more determined. After all, she was older than John—more grown up.

Then the unexpected happened. Mom came home. Mercilessly she lit into her husband. "What on God's green earth are you thinking? Teaching our own children to smoke!"

As soon as possible he got her aside and explained his theory. While accepting the fact that he was sincere in his objective, she was unconvinced that it would work and remained infuriated with him.

Of course time healed the rift, but still more time did something further. Dad's scheme today, two decades later, seems well validated. Ann and John, now out of the nest and married, will allow no tobacco in their homes!

LEARNING EARLY

The Fourth of July parade was in progress. The streets were lined with spectators with many children sitting on the curbs. Charly, age four, was very attentive to the little girl sitting beside him, and before the festivities were ended, he was hugging and kissing her. His parents, standing nearby, were a bit awed.

"Who's the little friend you sat next to?" his mother asked as the trio walked home.

"I dunno."

"You don't know? But you were hugging and kissing her?"

"Uh-huh."

"Well, did you like her all that much?"

"No, I didn't like her."

"You didn't like her?" The mother's voice clearly showed astonishment. "Then how come you were hugging and kissing her?"

"She had gum drops."

(Recently I had occasion to visit in the home of Charly and his parents. The boy is seventeen now and it is his chore to clean house on Saturdays. Charly has a girl. He does like her this time, but would you care to guess who helps Charly clean house on Saturday? Yes, I did get the proper title for this story!)

LENGTHY PROBLEM

A story similar to this has been around for years, but Bill Daggett, a retired manual training teacher in Long Beach, California, claims this actually happened in his class some years ago.

A little Mexican boy came to him with a problem.

The lad held up a piece of one by four lumber about thirty inches long. "Mr. Daggett," he said with worry showing in his big brown eyes, "I've cut this board off twice and it still isn't long enough."

LESSON IN MOTIVATION

It was decades ago when the roads were pure mud and the main form of human transportation (other than on trains and walking) was by horse and buggy.

"Walter's father said to the lad one afternoon, "Walter, you'd better wash the buggy today."

"Aw gee, Dad," the boy replied. "What's the use? It'll just get dirty again."

"What's that, Son?"

"What's the use of washing the buggy? It'll just get dirty again."

"Well, now, let's see; you're probably right, and according to that theory, you don't need to come in to supper tonight, 'cause you'll just get hungry again!"

When Walter came in to supper that night, the buggy was clean.

LET'S SEE THE EVIDENCE, DAD

Before super markets, there were markets. More explicitly, there were grocery stores, butcher shops and "markets."

Younger readers might not be aware that several decades ago, in many cities there was a central market, usually "downtown," and often referred to as the "city market." Here were several booths, individually operated, where fruits, vegetables and other farm produce were available. Most every family would go to the market occasionally, perhaps once a week.

A four-year-old knows little about the world of finance; he or she is more concerned with important things, such as marbles, tops, dolls, dogs, frogs, tricycles, etc., etc.

However, when the crash in stock prices struck in 1929, children were subjected to a deluge of adult conversation about the catastrophe.

During this hectic period, Jimmy went with his family, as was the weekly custom, to the city market. With arms full of purchases, the group was now heading back to the car when Jimmy made a suggestion.

"Daddy," the child said, "can't we go see where the bottom dropped out of the market?"

LIBERATED WOMAN

Seated in the restaurant and waiting for dinner, Lynn, age three, decided she should go to the restroom. As her mother made a move to go with her, it was "No, no, I'm big enough to go by myself."

"Are you sure you can find it? Are you sure you can find the right one?"

Yes, the child was sure. Nevertheless, the mother wrote on a piece of paper the words, "Women" and "Ladies," and gave it to the child saying, "The room you'll want will have one of these words on the door."

In three or four minutes the child returned, and she asked, "How'd you make out? Okay?"

"Sure, there was a real nice man in there!"

The mother gulped, then, regained her composure. "Oh, Honey, you must have had the wrong room. Didn't you use that piece of paper I gave you?"

"No, there weren't words, there were just pictures." Still a bit unsettled, the mother said, "Come, you show me." They went through the hall marked "Rest Rooms." Lynn pointed to the picture on the first door they came to and said, "See, I went in here."

"Oh, but Honey, can't you see, this is the men's room. You can tell because in the picture the man is wearing pants."

"Well, gee Mommy, you're not a man and you're wearing pants!"

LINGUISTIC SHORT CUT

Measles were in epidemic proportions, and Russell had been severely restricted in the children that he could play with. One child, however, having had the affliction when he was an infant was considered "safe," so he was allowed to come to Russell's house for the afternoon. The following conversation between the pair was overheard:

"What is measles, anyway?" the visiting boy asked.

"It's a sickness," Russell replied.

"I've been sick before and I could play with other kids."

"Well, this sickness is different," Russell explained.

"What's different about it?"

"It's the *German* measles."

"What's the difference about German measles?"

"Well, I'm not sure, but I think you get red spots all over you just like other measles, but then you start to speak German."

"Ich glaube Ich habe die masern!"

LOOKING FOR THE SILVER LINING

Tracie, age seven, and her brother, Frankie, age nine, both hated spinach. Since they were not otherwise too fussy about food, their parents seldom had the disfavored greens, but they were very strict about "cleaning up your plate." They were careful not to overload the children's plates, and, of course, there were exceptions if the child did not feel well, etc.

Came the time the family visited the father's parents in Norfolk, and Grandpa took them to his fancy club for lunch.

The children were awed by the splendor of the large dining room, the table beautifully set, the plush carpet.

A chicken breast with baked potato in the half shell was offered. Both children liked chicken, and the rest sounded interesting so they ordered it, giving no particular thought regarding what else might be served with the entrée.

When their lunch came—you've guessed it—there was a generous helping of spinach on the plate. The greens were chopped as opposed to stringy, and in the center there was a little crater with a dab of butter.

Tracie was obviously jolted by this turn of events. Her eyes dwelt a moment on the spinach. Then she looked at Frankie, caught his eye and noted his expression which was as wry as her own. Then her eyes surveyed anew the elaborate surroundings, the dark red ceiling-to-floor draperies, the dazzling chandeliers, the deep, soft, maroon carpet, the gold braid on the waiter's red jacket. Her gaze went again to her plate, and then once more to her brother's eyes. Then she leaned toward him and whispered, "Do you suppose it'll taste better in here?"

LOOK IT UP, MOM

Dorothy's mother taught a class in family relations. The group of parents met regularly in her home to learn the arts of better promoting family harmony.

As often happens when a parent is engrossed on some project, Dorothy, at age six, often felt a bit left out, and it was on an afternoon when the child came home from school and particularly wanted to communicate with her mother.

Seeing her mother engaged in speaking to a dozen or more women in the living room, the child was able to muster a bit of patience, but not for long.

Soon, she tried meagerly to get her mother's attention, but to no avail. Her mother kept right on with the discourse, alternately reading from a book on child psychology, then laying the volume aside to comment or ask for discussion on some relevant point.

Dorothy fidgeted, growing increasingly impatient as her mother proceeded full steam ahead with her endeavor. Further frustrated, the child now tried to summon her mother aside, beckoning with her hand, but she was ignored.

Dorothy proceeded to a landing in the stairway which was four steps above where the group was gathered, and there, off to the right of where her mother stood, but in direct view of the other ladies, proceeded to stand on her head.

Not noticing the action, but seeing an amazed expression spread over the faces of her audience, Dorothy's mother turned to see the spectacle, and just as she did, the child, still totally inverted, asked, "Well, Mother dear, what does your stupid book say to do about this?"

LOVE ON PROBATION

No mother would deny that her child occasionally "gets in her hair!" Three-year-old Mark had been out of sorts all day. It seemed that he and his mother were at odds on every issue. He complained about his food and threw it on the floor. The toys that were supposed to be kept in his room were left strewn about the house and his mother harped at him to pick them up.

The child resisted every step of the way as she put him down for his nap. Finally she gave him a swat on the bottom and he seemed to settle down. She leaned over and kissed him, said, "I love you," left the room and closed the door.

A moment later the door opened and Mark called out, "I love you, Mom, but I sure don't like you very much right now!"

LOVE POTION

Four-year-old Jerome and his Pomeranian, Angel, were inseparable.

One day the boy's mother found the cover off the butter dish. Thinking the boy had made himself a snack, she replaced the cover and thought no more about it. However, this began to occur frequently; still, she gave it no serious thought. Then finally she discovered the boy dipping his finger in the butter and smearing it on his cheek.

Surprised, she said to the boy, "Jerome, what are you doing? Putting butter on your face? What on earth are you doing that for?"

"'Cuz Angel likes it; he gives me lots of kisses!"

LUCRATIVE CAREER

Ty was watching a football game on television when his uncle arrived for a visit.

"Hey, Ty," the uncle teased, "you going to spend your whole life watching TV? You'll never grow up to amount to anything if you do that."

"That's not so, you can learn lots of stuff on TV."

"Stuff like what? What can you learn by watching that boob tube?"

"Well, right now it's helping teach me what I'm going to be when I grow up."

"Yeah, and what's that?" the uncle asked, prodding.

"I'm going to be a cowboy, that's what!"

"Big deal, Ty's going to be a cowboy. I'll tell you one thing, young fella; you'll never make any money being a cowboy!"

But the uncle found himself unequal to the lad's question:

"A *Dallas* Cowboy?"

MADE BEFORE FORKS

Kellie had been with her grandparents for a week and now her grandma was driving her back to Richmond. The child was sitting up against her grandmother as they drove.

"Gee, Grandma," Kellie said, "those are sure nice earrings you're wearing."

"Yes, I like them; do you like dangly earrings, Honey?"

"Yeah, they're real pretty. Where'd you get them?"

"I traded with your great aunt Susie for them."

"What did you trade her?"

"I traded her some silver for these earrings and this bracelet." She held her hand over toward the child, showing her the wrist piece.

"You made a good trade, Grandma."

"You think so, eh?"

"Yeah, you sure did. You got beautiful stuff, and besides you can always eat with your fingers!"

MAGIC CHEF

When Julie was vacationing at her grandmother's home, the latter was obligated to go to a dinner meeting, and a neighbor who had taken a liking to the child invited her to dinner.

After dinner Julie and her host and hostess had played Parcheesi with the youngster winning.

Julie excitedly and proudly reported this to her grandmother along with the less important events of the evening.

"And what did you have for dinner?" Grandma asked.

"Chicken."

"Fried?"

"Uh huh."

"What else?"

"Oh, potatoes."

"What kind?"

"White."

"Yes, I know, but how were they cooked?"

"Fine."

MALE CHAUVINISM

The class was discussing the changes that take place in humans as they grow from birth to maturity.

"We all grow hair on our heads from the time we're born," the teacher said. Then, addressing Tim, she asked, "but tell me what will happen when you get to be thirteen or fourteen?"

"I'll start growing hair on my chin, and I'll be able to shave like my dad."

"Right," the teacher responded.

"I can hardly wait till I'm able to shave like my dad," Tim added with enthusiasm.

Tim turned to Juliana, "I'll bet you can hardly wait till you're your dad's age so you can shave your chin too, hey, Juliana?" he asked beaming.

"No, of course not, silly; I can hardly wait till I'm my mom's age so I can shave my legs. Boys! Geeeeeee!!!"

MARVEL OF THE AIRWAYS

Scottie had never been close to a pregnant woman, that is, not close enough to notice. There were fat people and not-so-fat people, and he let it go at that.

However, one day he accompanied his mother to the beauty parlor, and it happened that the operator who worked on his mother's hair was close to delivery.

When they departed, Scottie said to his mother, "Gee, Mom wasn't that lady awfully fat?"

"Oh, she's going to have a baby. The baby's in her tummy. It grows there till it is completely formed and big and healthy enough to be born, and then it'll be delivered by the mother into the outside world."

This seemed to satisfy the child and nothing more was said.

A few days later, Scottie and his father were in the yard and an airplane flew overhead.

"Daddy, Daddy, Daddy, look! Look at the airplane!"

His father looked skyward, saw the plane, noticed that it was outfitted with bulky radar equipment.

"See," the child continued, "the airplane's going to have a baby!"

MASQUERADE BRIDGE PARTY

Jim was visiting his grandmother, and it was her turn to entertain the bridge club so she said to the lad, "Jim, maybe you'd like to go to the movies this afternoon. You probably wouldn't have much fun around here; I have some girls coming in for bridge."

"Girls? Oh, yeah, I know what you mean," the boy said, "You mean the girls with the old lady faces!"

MATHEMATICAL DILEMMA

Elixia had been having trouble getting to sleep. A school chum made a suggestion to her, which she decided to try. She met with some degree of success, but one night her daddy came into her room to adjust the window; as he tiptoed out, she began to cry.

"Honey, I'm sorry," he said, "I tried to be quiet. I'm sorry if I frightened you."

"Well, you didn't scare me, but I was counting sheep and you made me lose my place!"

MATHEMATICAL SLIP-UP

Grandma Krummi was proud of her Finnish heritage. In America, her children, busy growing up among different ethnic groups, fell away from many of the Finnish traditions.

Now that she had grandchildren, she was anxious that some facets of her heritage be preserved in her descendants, so she frequently told her grandchildren stories about her early life in Finland, and, whenever she could, encouraged them to learn a bit of the Finnish history, customs, traditions, etc.

One day, Tyler, her three-year-old grandson was playing with his Weebles. He had one on each finger of his left hand. With his right index finger, he was pointing to his left hand and counting. "One Weeble, two Weebles, three Weebles, four Weebles, five Weebles."

"Tyler," his grandmother asked, "can you count in Finn?"

"Sure, I can."

"Okay, let me hear you count in Finn."

"Okay, one Finn, two Finns, three Finns, four Finns—!"

MATTER OF LIFE AND DEATH

At age four, Kelley had spent the summer with her grandparents on their farm some hundred miles away. After returning home, she missed the animals and the interesting and eventful life in the country and was not adverse to engaging her imagination in ploys aimed at enabling her to return to her grandparents.

In a telephone conversation she told her grandma: "I'm trapped here—just—just—I'm just trapped!"

"What do you mean, trapped? What's trapping you?"

"A big monster; he's right here, right now and he's got me trapped."

"Oh, sure, and I suppose you want me to come and get you?"

"Yes, and you'd better hurry if you ever want to see me again. He's getting ready to eat me up!"

MEETING IN THE BY-AND-BY

The goldfish was floating belly-up and Tyler went screaming to his grandmother. "Grandma," he cried, "come quick, something's wrong with Daisy!"

"Well, Honey," she said, after examining the fish, "I don't know how it happened, but I'm afraid she's dead."

Tyler began to sob. "Don't cry, Honey," Grandma said, "these things happen, and I'm sure Daisy will go to heaven."

Not long after that, Grandma was going on an errand, and she asked Tyler if he would like to go along.

Trying to start the car, Grandma exclaimed, "Oh, gee, the battery's shot!"

"Who do you think shot it, Grandma?" the child asked.

"No, no, I just mean the battery's dead."

"Oh, you mean it's dead like Daisy? Now will it go to heaven and be with Daisy?"

MELODY OF LOVE

"Dudley," five-year-old Mary said, addressing her older brother, "how can you like toads and frogs? They're icky."

"They're fun." Dudley responded.

"All they do is grunt and croak," Mary continued. "Birds and flowers and butterflies are much more beautiful."

"Birds and flowers are sissy stuff. Frogs and lizards and fish are for men."

"Oh, ick!"

"Okay," Dudley shot back, "I'll like what I like and you like what you like."

"I don't just *like* flowers and birds; I love them!"

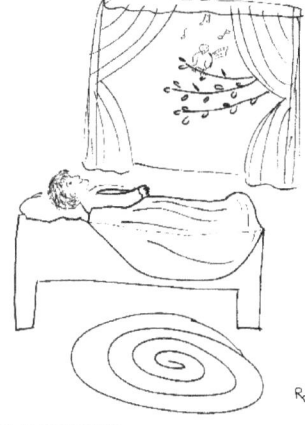

"Okay, but they don't love you back!"

"Oh, yes, they do. At least the birds do."

"How do you know that? How can you tell birds love you?"

"Because, smarty, the robins sit outside my window every morning and sing, 'dearie, dearie, dearie.'"

MICHAEL, YOU SHOULD HAVE WHISTLED

Michael was six. David, his eight-year-old brother had received for his birthday a pair of pajamas with the image of a skeleton on them.

From that moment on, there was no peace; Michael had to have a similar pair.

While his constant bugging caused his mother a degree of annoyance, it did solve a problem for her, because Michael's birthday was only a few days off.

When Michael opened his package, he was, of course, delighted. Not only did he like the gift, but there had been the usual problem of the younger sibling keeping up with his older brother, and now he had moved a step toward equality.

However, although Michael had observed David in his pajamas, he evidently was not aware of the luminous quality which caused the skeleton to stand out from the rest of the garment in the dark.

Of course, he had to wear the pajamas the first night. About midnight his parents heard an earsplitting scream. They rushed to his room. Michael was sitting on the side of his bed whimpering.

"Darling, what's wrong? What's the matter?" his mother asked anxiously.

"I – I – I got up to go to the bathroom and I saw myself in the mirror and I scared me!"

MINE FIELD

It was two weeks before Christmas, and shoppers were streaming through the toy store. My friend observed a mother with two small children, a girl and a boy.

The boy picked up a squeaky toy and pumped it rapidly, producing the intended noise.

"Put that back," commanded the mother as she gave the boy a whack on the cheek.

A bit further on, the girl picked up a doll and started to take off its dress. The woman slapped the girl as she had the boy, demanding sharply, "Put that back."

A toy machine gun proved too much for the boy. He picked it up, aimed it at my friend and pulled the trigger. The sharp "rat-a-tat-tat" startled the mother, and she swung around and cuffed the boy severely on the mouth, fairly yelling, "Put that back!"

The lad dropped the gun and walked swiftly away, saying "I'm going back to the car; it's too dangerous in here!"

MISUNDERSTOOD GESTURE

Carl handed the sealed note from his kindergarten teacher to his mother.

"What's this?" his mother asked.

"I don't know," the child said as he made a hasty retreat and joined his playmates on the vacant lot adjacent to his home.

Mother opened the envelope and studied the note, then sat down to give some thought to the problem the note posed.

"Carl," she called, "you come in here, I want to talk to you."

"I can't now, I'm on second base."

"Second base will just have to wait. You come in here, and you come in here now!"

"Carl, you sit down," his mother said when he was inside. "We need to talk. I want to know, have you been sassing your teacher?"

"No."

"Well, this note from Miss Clawson says you have been sassing her. I don't think she'd go to all the trouble of sending me a note telling me you've been sassing her if you have not. Now, I'll ask you once more, have you been sassing your teacher?"

"Well, maybe just a little bit."

"Now, how long has this been going on? How many times have you sassed her?"

"Well, just once."

"I don't think she'd be sending me a note if you had just sassed her once. I think she'd just tell you not to do that anymore. Teachers try to correct these little problems with the children themselves, and usually only bother the parents if the child continues to misbehave. Now how many times have you sassed her?"

"I don't know."

"Did you stick your tongue out at her?"

"No."

"But this note," she held up the paper, "says you did."

Carl looked down, didn't reply immediately, then, "Oh, well, yes, I did once, but I was just showing her my tongue so she could see I wasn't sick!"

"MODERN ART"

That Mom and Dad took a very dim view of so-called "modern art" was anything but a secret. They never failed to express their disgust when viewing a grotesque sculpture or crazy mixed up painting.

They took five-year-old Inez when they went for the first time to the new city hall. Outside on the lawn stood a structure, if you could call it That, approximately twenty feet high. It was a mass of iron rods put together so as to form a design which, although symmetrical, seemed not particularly pleasing to the three as they stood there gazing at it.

"Maybe that's something beautiful," Dad commented, "but I must say it doesn't do anything for me."

"Oh, yes it does," Mom interjected, "it has relieved you of some of your tax money. Man, if that isn't a pile of junk, I never saw one!"

They were silent a moment, then Inez, evidently feeling that she ought to contribute something to the conversation, said, "Gee, we have a spider on our trellis that does a better job than that!"

MORE IMPORTANTLY EMPLOYED

Three-year-old Mark had come tumbling down the stairs. He was crying and screaming, and Mom came running and picked him up.

She rocked him a while as she looked for any serious bruises or injury. Finally the sobs subsided somewhat, and the child lay limp and whimpering in her arms.

"Honey, you have to be careful when you come down the stairs," she said. "Why weren't you holding on to the railing?"

"I couldn't."

"You couldn't? Why couldn't you?"

"Cuz my thumb was in my mouth."

MORTAL OVERSIGHT

It was obvious that Donny, five years old, had been listening to the adult conversations. He didn't understand everything he heard which became obvious when he attempted to comment on the matter being discussed by his mother and a neighbor lady.

They were discussing the passing of another neighbor and his mother was saying that it was so terribly sad that the widow was left with three children who had adored their father.

"Well,' said Donny, "it was his own fault."

His mother turned and asked, "What do you mean, it was his own fault?"

"It was his own fault he died," the youngster answered.

"What do you mean, it was his own fault he died?"

"It was his own fault. He died because he didn't buy any life insurance!"

MR. BUHLER'S SUDDEN DEFLATION

Mr. Buhler was nine-year-old Wally's counselor. One day Wally came to him and said, "Mr. Buhler, we had to write a story about our hero, and you know I just thought and thought and thought, and I couldn't think of anybody to write about, so I wrote about you."

Mr. Buhler chuckled to himself and then said, "Well, now, Wally, I think that's nice. Really, I'm rather honored."

"Well, yeah, Mr. Buhler, but I only got a 'C' on it!"

NAVIGATIONAL CONSULTANT

Five-year-old Ted was up to his old tricks of lording it over his younger sister who was three. He felt it his duty to know everything about everything as often the older child is inclined to do.

A fishing trip was in the making and Dad asked Ted to put the anchor in the boat. The lad was puffing a bit and scowling as he lifted the heavy weight over into the bow of the boat, and thus did not respond with the greatest of patience when Betty, his sister, asked, "What's an anchor for?"

"Oh, ya dumb kid," came the answer, "that's what you use to make the boat don't go!"

NEW MUTATION

This episode occurred back in the days when fresh produce was not as widely shipped as it is today. Corn on the cob for the most part was eaten only in the summer. It was not found in grocery stores out of season, nor were there home freezers for the preservation of food stuffs.

Fresh sweet corn was a special favorite of Carl, age six, and although canned corn was available, it seemed his family so thoroughly enjoyed the fresh product that they did not bother with canned corn at other times of the year.

Carl's aunt and uncle lived on a farm and canned a good deal of the produce they raised. Carl was invited to stay with them for a spring weekend, and when he returned home he was reporting to his parents about the visit. His mother asked him if his aunt was a good cook.

"Yeah, she sure is," was the reply. "She sure had some good stuff. We even had corn on the cob off the cob!"

NEW TRICK OF THE TRADE

Five-year-old Mark went fishing with his dad. For a while they had some action, but no keepers; all the fish were small. Soon, even that stopped. As Mark's interest waned, he ceased paying attention to his bobber.

"Mark," his father said," you've got to watch your bobber."

"I am, Dad," was the disinterested response. But the boy gave his attention to other sundry matters. He fiddled with the oarlock, spinning it in its holder.

"Mark, watch your bobber," his dad said.

"I am, Dad."

The lad took the landing net and swished it back and forth in the water.

"Mark," his dad said, now using a little stiffer tone, "if you're going to be a fisherman, you've got to watch your bobber."

"I am, Dad, I am."

Soon the boy was toying with the minnow bucket. He pulled it above the water's surface, opened the lid and peered in.

"Mark," his dad seemed thoroughly disgusted now, and he ordered the child in no uncertain terms, "you settle down now and you watch your bobber!"

"I am, Dad, I am. I'm trickin' the fish. I'm watchin' the bobber out of the corner of my eye!"

NEXT TIME, GO TO HIM FIRST!

Off and on, Mary Beth had expressed a desire for a real skirt, a skirt like what moms and older girls wear. In two weeks she'd be starting kindergarten, and her desire for the more feminine attire came into sharp focus.

As her mother prepared her for the new experience, the child intensified her campaign. *She wanted a skirt*, and there was no foolin' about it!

No hour of the day could slip by without some mention of the need for a skirt, and the "need" and therefore the "mention" grew greater by the day.

On the Friday before Labor Day, Mom took her to the mall, and there, wonder of wonders, bought the child her first skirt.

The child was ecstatic. When Dad arrived home that evening, she proudly modeled the new garment for him.

Seated at the dinner table, Dad said, "Mary Beth, I'll call on you to say grace tonight."

"Dear Heavenly Father, we thank thee for this food and for our family and all our blessings and for having my mommy get me a new skirt so I won't have to fuss at her about it ever again!"

NINE POINT NINE ON THE RICHTER SCALE

Everything seemed normal in the Montessori classroom of preschoolers until the teacher noticed that Nathan wasn't his usual bubbly self. "Nathan, what's the matter? Aren't you feeling well?" the teacher asked.

"No," was the simple answer.

The teacher took his temperature. It was 100.3. She told the child to lie down and rest and that she would call his parents. Soon he started shaking, stopped breathing and turned blue.

Responding to the teacher's 911 call, the paramedics were on the scene within three minutes.

After the paramedics departed with the child, the teacher told the children to sit down and she explained to them just what had happened, told them it was a seizure, but that Nathan would be all right, and that it had happened to him before, a fact she learned when she had phoned Nathan's mother. She told the children they could ask any questions that occurred to them.

"Is it contagious?" "Could I get it if I got a fever?" "Will Nathan come back to school?" "Will he remember us?" "Why was he blue?"

When the children left school that day, they were rather subdued, but they were very orderly. The teacher concluded that everything had been explained to them properly.

She was a bit surprised a few days later when Libby's mother advised that her daughter had reported the event as follows: "Nathan had an earthquake!"

NO CANNIBAL, SHE

Ever since Maarit, as a tiny girl, had a ride on a horse, she had been absolutely captivated by the animals. She had been raised in Finland but visited the United States when she was nine.

Whether gelatin is not common in Finland or whether her family simply did not use it is not clear, but when seeing it for the first time on the dinner table of her U.S. hostess, she asked what it was. The hostess explained that it was made from horses' hooves (although there are also other sources).

The dinner progressed normally, but the hostess observed that the child had not touched the gelatin.

"Maarit," the hostess asked a bit surprised, thinking surely the girl would try the food since she had asked about it, "you haven't even tasted your gelatin. Aren't you even going to try it?"

"No," the child responded, "I don't eat my friends!"

NO CAUSE TO PANIC

The amusement in this episode lies in the fact that little Billy Foster, six, really thought he was providing an adequate answer.

His mother's sister had come to visit, bringing her toddler, Lucy, who was the approximate age of Billy's little brother, Henry.

The two sisters had not seen each other for two years and were deeply engrossed in "catching up." Suddenly Mrs. Foster realized she hadn't seen her little one for a quarter hour and that he perhaps had wandered off down the street as he sometimes did if not restrained.

Anxiously, she cried out, "Where's Henry?"

"Oh, he's with Lucy," Billy replied calmly.

"Where's Lucy?" asked the frantic mother.

"She's with Henry!"

NO FROGS

Bedlam had prevailed while the family was getting settled in their new house in the country. Nine-year-old Chad was delighted with the move as he now had the opportunity to enjoy a whole new type of outdoor activity.

On the back of the property was a small creek, which held a fascination for the boy. About a week after the family moved in, the boy's mother discovered in their aquarium, in addition to the goldfish:

-20 salamanders

-9 blue belly lizards

-5 alligator lizards

-1 eleven-inch garter snake

"What on earth?" the mother screamed. "Chad, you come here this instant! What on earth are you thinking of? An aquarium is no place for those slimy things! I'm off to the store, and you see to it that when I get back, those things are out of there!"

Back from shopping, Mom checked the aquarium. The "things" were gone. Good!

"Chad," she called.

"Yeah, Mom," came the reply.

"Where are you?"

"I'm in here, in the bath tub."

Good boy; got rid of the filthy "things" and was now washing off the slime. Yuck! Good boy!

She went in the bathroom. Sure enough, Chad was in the tub.

And so were:

-20 salamanders

-9 blue belly lizards

-5 alligator lizards

-1 eleven-inch garter snake

NO GLUTTON, HE

Four-year-old Dennis asked, "Mommy, can I have a chee?"

"A chee? I guess I don't know what you're talking about."

"A chee, Mommy, a chee, can I have a chee?"

"You'll have to explain what you mean; I don't know what you mean by a 'chee'."

"You keep it in the refrigerator."

His mother went to the refrigerator, opened the door and said, "Show me; show me what you're talking about."

"There, right there," Dennis said, pointing to one of the little covers in the refrigerator door.

"Oh, you mean cheese," his mother exclaimed.

"Yes, but I only want one!"

NO HONEY, THAT WAS THE ATCHISON, TOPEKA AND THE SANTA FE

Grandma had proved very apt at potty training the first two grandchildren, so guess what? You guessed it, she fell heir to the job when Renea, number three, attained the appropriate age.

At various times, Renea had heard mention of the fact that Grandma did the potty training, but she had not grasped the concept, and knew only that this was something that Grandma had done with her older brother and sister.

When Grandma came for a visit, Renea understood that the elder would be taking her back to her home to potty train her, but even then she really did not know what was involved.

In route to Grandma's house, they encountered a railroad crossing where the bell was ringing as the barricade was being lowered, and Grandma brought the car to a halt. Soon the freight train with its three thundering locomotives approached. Renea was awed and delighted. There were many cars and it took several minutes for them to pass.

When finally the highway was clear, the barricade lifted and the bell ceased its clanging. Slowly the click-clack, click-clack diminished as the caboose shrank into the distance. Grandma shifted gears and proceeded across the track.

"Was that it, Grandma?" Renea asked.

"Was that what, Honey?"

"Was that the potty train?"

NONPRODUCTIVE ACTIVITY

An example of infinity might be a list of reasons children give for not going to bed or for getting up after retiring.

Sometimes the small fry drop off into slumber land the second they get horizontal, but then there are the other times.

Audra, age five, was restless, and had pretty well exhausted the old standbys: "I have to go to the bathroom." "I'm thirsty." "I just remembered something I have to tell you." "I had to see if I put my homework in my folder."

The next time up, she appeared in the living room and when her impatient mother harshly demanded to know, "What on earth is it this time?"

"Well, I thought I heard you call me."

"I did not call, now for the last time, you get back in that bed and not another peep, not one peep!"

"But, Mother," the child responded, starting to cry, "it's so boring. All you do is lie there!"

NOT A BAD IDEA

Tim and Melanie had been playing around with masking tape and in fun they stuck a piece over their mouths.

Mom was preparing to go to the supermarket. "Come on now," she said to the children, "get those silly things off your faces. We're going to the store."

At the super market, Mom performed the dual chores of selecting items for purchase and keeping the young ones corralled.

At the checkout counter, she became absorbed in the tallying process. She was vaguely aware of a slight commotion and giggling behind her but now was tendering her money and did not turn to observe the children.

When her transaction was completed, Mom did turn, only to find that Tim and Melanie again had the tape plastered over their faces covering their mouths.

She was about to speak, to order the tapes removed, but before she could do so, her eyes fell on the face of a woman in the adjacent line. There was a broad grin on the latter's face and she said, "I do declare, I've got a couple of livewires myself, and it's often crossed my mind to do just what you've done!"

NOT BY ANY OTHER NAME

Every teacher wonders sometimes whether it is all worthwhile, and then...

It was the last day of school, and Nicole had brought Miss Charlotte a present. It was a long, narrow box, and the teacher exclaimed, "Oh, has someone brought me a posy?"

"No, it's better than that!"

Miss Charlotte opened the box and lifted out the green tissue. Gently she felt its contents, almost in a caressing fashion, purposely prolonging the process so that the child might sense and share her delight.

"Are you sure someone hasn't brought me a flower?" Miss Charlotte asked.

"No, it's better than a flower!"

Slowly the teacher unfolded the paper, but just before the contents became visible, the child found it impossible to keep the secret longer and exploded.

"It's better than a flower, it's a rose!"

NOTHING, REALLY

They were at it again, squabbling – Mary Ann, age four, and her younger sister, Susan. Suddenly the latter began crying and screaming.

"Mary Ann," their mother called anxiously, "what did you do to your sister?"

Quickly and boldly came the reply: "Hit her, slap her, pinch her, scratch her, bit her, kick her and pull her hair was all I did to her!"

NO TIME FOR UNDERLINGS

The parents of nine-year-old Chris and seven-year-old Missy, although faithful Episcopalians, found it advisable to have the children attend a Catholic school, and thus they became as familiar with the "Hail Mary" as they had been with "Our Father."

The family had a small yacht on an inland river, and one day while sailing they saw storm clouds gathering. They quickly lowered the sail and, using the engine, hurried to a protective cove. The wind came suddenly and fiercely as the sky darkened with swirling clouds, strongly suggestive of tornadoes.

The whole family took refuge under a table in the main salon, and, as the craft pitched and tossed furiously, the father exclaimed, "This is serious; we'd best all pray!"

Chris started, "Hail Mary, full of Grace—," but Missy promptly interrupted, "No, Chris, no, there isn't time. We gotta go direct to God Himself!"

NOT SO SECRET WEAPON

How, at the tender age of three, she knew, is a mystery, but, that she knew is a certainty. Yes, she was dead right in her appraisal, which is summed up in the two final words of this anecdote.

Julie was staying with Grandma, and Grandma was preparing for a date. The elder had just showered and now was fussing before the mirror as the fairer sex (thank goodness) is prone to do.

Julie, just barely able to see the top of the vanity, was scanning the various weapons being employed in this preparation for the feminine offensive. Her eyes fell on a piece of fabric, shiny black, lacy, with two little bright red bows.

Wide eyed, she pointed to the object asking, "What's that?"

Thinking she was replying on a plane of innocence, Grandma said, "Those are my undies."

Julie glanced at grandma's face, then again at the black garment. Her grin (and remember she's only three) reflected a bit of amusement, a bit of accusation. She waggled a finger toward Grandma and said, "Naughty girl!"

NOT TOO SUBTLE BLACKMAIL

Last year Freddie had expressed some skepticism about the Santa Claus business. Now he was pretty well convinced.

"You guys, you and Mom, are Santa Claus, aren't you?" he asked his dad.

"What makes you think that?"

"Well, I know he couldn't get down a chimney with all that stuff or go all over the world in one night. You've been fooling us."

"Well, don't spoil it for your brother. At only three, Jackie can enjoy Santa Claus for several more Christmases."

"Yeah, but you've always told me I should tell the truth, so why shouldn't I tell him that you and Mom are Santa Claus? That's the truth, isn't it?"

"Well, in a way, yes. But can't you continue to believe in the spirit of Santa Claus? Maybe there's no real such person. Maybe the parents actually get the presents and put them under the tree, but when they do it they're filled with the Santa Claus spirit. Is that so hard to accept?"

"Well, maybe not, but why shouldn't I tell Jackie what's true?"

"There's no need to, really. Just don't tell him; let him believe and enjoy what Santa puts under the tree."

"Well, okay, maybe I wouldn't tell him if I'd happen to find a ten-speed bike under the tree!"

OBEDIENCE TO THE LETTER

Jerry was constantly getting in trouble in school for talking too much, and it wasn't only in school. He was something of a pest in the way he was always talking. Also, he often spoke without making too much sense, as though talking was the important thing, the subject matter was secondary.

He was frequently admonished for this, told not to interrupt, and told not to talk so much. He would remember and comply for a while, but soon be right back to the habit.

One day his mother sat him down and said. "Now Jerry, I want to have a serious talk with you. We've told you that you talk too much. If you'd think before you speak you wouldn't talk so much, and then when you do speak, you'll make more sense, people will understand what you say, and you won't get in trouble at school. Now I want you to think and think and think each time before you speak."

As always, he pleasantly agreed to do better. "Yes, Mother," he said, "I'll remember."

The next day was very cold and windy, with cool drafts stirring throughout the house and family members were standing close to the fireplace to keep warm.

Suddenly Jerry pointed to his aunt and said excitedly, "Aunt Martha, I think, I think, I think your dress tail is on fire!"

OF DOGS, FISH AND GUNS

When the guide arrived at the resort, his clients had their fishing tackle all assembled and were ready to go.

"I'm Sparkey," the guide said, extending his hand.

"And I'm Ted, this is Mrs. Miller, and this is our son, Mark."

Mark was bubbling. "We wanna go catch a huskie, Sparkey," he said enthusiastically.

"You mean muskie," the guide corrected, "well, we'll do our best."

The group caught a few walleyes, a few bass, but no muskie. It was a congenial group, and when the guide dropped the trio off at their resort at four o'clock, he said, "If you'd like, we might try it for a little while this evening. I can pick you up again about seven fifteen."

At the appointed hour, the Millers were assembled on the dock. Mark was raring to go. "Come on, Sparkey, let's go." He said. "Let's go get a musket this time!"

OFF COLOR STORY

Little Connie recently had learned about color blindness and one day declared. "Mommy, I think I'm color blind!"

"What on earth makes you say that?"

"'Cause Grandma's thumb looks just like everybody else's to me, but you and Aunt Millie keep saying it's green!"

OF MICE AND SMALL BOYS

Three-year-old Chris had been out in the barn with his father. When they returned to the house, the child said to his mother, "Hey, Mom, I saw two mouses out in the barn."

"You did? Gee, those cats must not be doing their job. But, listen Honey, you don't say 'mouses.' You say 'mouse' when it's one mouse, but if there are two, you say 'mice.'"

The child pondered a moment, then said, "Oh I get it. If it's one mouse, it's a mouse, if it's two mouses, it's mice. Well then, if it's three mouses, it must be a rat!"

ON WELFARE

The Montessori school was on an acreage where the owner-teacher lived. Early in the school year, she took her pupils on a walk around the grounds, showing them the various facilities, and, what intrigued the children most, the animals—horses, pigs, ducks, rabbits, etc.

When April came, another walk outside was taken to enable the children to enjoy the spring growth, the budding shrubs, the blossoms, etc. At the conclusion of the outing, Rose, a little four-year-old whose family was vegetarian, asked, "But Mrs. George, where are the pigs?"

"Oh, they're bacon now, and pork chops; they're in our freezer."

That night at home Rose pleaded with her mother, "Oh, Mommy, can't we please take some food over to Mrs. George. They're so poor—they even had to eat their pigs!"

OPERATION DISINFECT

As happens in many families from time to time, a youngster may bring home an unsavory word or remark which is picked up at school or on the street whereupon the parents threaten to "wash out your mouth with soap."

Eventually it happened in the Greer family. Eleven-year-old Carl could not resist the urge to "test," and father Greer could not resist the urge to follow through.

Seven-year-old Bertha watched the procedure in silence as her brother squirmed, spit, cried, and promised never to do it again. She gave not the slightest indication, either by word or expression, as to what her inner reaction might be.

However, a few days later she accompanied her dad when he took the family car to have some repairs made on the exhaust system. The mechanic had the usual struggles disconnecting and refitting the segments, and, as reported on the side by father to mother Greer, used considerable "colorful" language during the process.

"Did you have fun, going with your dad to the garage?" Mrs. Greer asked the child.

"Yeah, but you know what, Mom?" was the reply, "I think I ought to have my ears washed out with soap!"

OPPORTUNITY OVERLOOKED

Paul was getting ready for school. Usually Benny stopped by and they both walked to school together, but Paul wasn't expecting Benny today.

Yesterday Benny had fallen victim to a flying baseball bat. The Blues had been playing the Chiefs, and the bat had slipped from Charley Cromwell's hands when he swung in a desperate but futile attempt to cinch the game.

Benny had to be taken to the hospital. He was examined; the wound was dressed, and he was released.

Paul was amazed when he answered the doorbell and found Benny standing there. Black and blue showed around the big bandage on his left upper forehead.

"Good gosh, you going to school today?" Paul asked.

"Sure, I'm okay, it doesn't even hurt."

"Well, my gosh, use it while you've gotta chance, dummy!"

ORIENTAL CUISINE

When Mauri learned that, due to a merger of her father's Japanese company and an American firm, her family would be moving from Japan to the United States, she was apprehensive to say the least. She had heard that distant lands were "strange," their people "different," and that adjustments for newcomers were difficult. It seemed to her she would have to live in a whole new world, new sights, new sounds, new tastes.

Upon landing at the Bradley International Airport, Mauri surveyed the facilities with interest. Well, not really too different from the Tokyo airport—more fair-skinned people proportionally, not much Japanese spoken, but not as shockingly different as she had feared.

One of her father's new business associates met them. He seemed like a nice guy and put her at ease by squatting to her height, smiling, and directing a few words specifically to her; it did not matter that she could not understand them.

As they drove from the airport, the child gazed intently at the passing scene. Suddenly her scanning eyes fell on two gold arches. She couldn't be sure. Breathlessly she waited till they were closer and she could be certain. Then she shrieked with delight, (translated) "Daddy, Mommy, look they have McDonald's over here too!"

OR MAYBE EVEN GOD!

The full Colonel of the Air Force stepped briskly from his base living quarters out onto the sidewalk. He was impeccably clad in dress blues. His white mustache was neatly trimmed and the bit of white hair that showed under his billed hat further enhanced his appearance of dignity.

Confronting him on the sidewalk were two tiny, blue-eyed, blonde angels, the daughters of a captain newly quartered nearby.

At such a vision of elegance, the girls' eyes widened.

"Are you a captain?" one girl asked.

"No," the Colonel replied.

The eyes grew even bigger. "Are you a – a – a Maaay-jor?"

"No."

The eyes almost popped out. This must be, indeed, a supreme personage.

And thus the final question:

"Are you a grandfather?"

OUT OF SIGHT—OUT OF MIND

It would be the first time Danielle had been left alone overnight in all her six years of existence. It would be the first time too, that her mom and dad had been on a holiday for the same period of time.

Danielle liked Mrs. Collins who would be staying with her during the five-day jaunt of the child's parents to Bermuda. Mrs. Collins drove the family to the airport. The goodbyes seemed normal enough; Danielle made no fuss.

"Now you be a good girl, and you do just what Mrs. Collins tells you to do."

"Okay, don't worry. I will, I will. G'bye, Mom; g'bye Dad," she said as she kissed them g'bye, "and have fun."

The plane had not yet reached cruising altitude before Mom began to worry. "You think she'll be all right?" she asked her husband.

"Of course, she'll be all right. She and Mrs. Collins get along fine."

Mom grew increasingly apprehensive. "We've never been away from her before, even overnight," she said when they were settled in their hotel.

"Don't worry. Don't worry. She'll be fine."

However, by the third night, Mom couldn't stand it any longer. "I just know she's dying of lonesomeness for us."

But each time she expressed her concern, her husband's reassurance showed a little more impatience.

Finally, her doubts got the best of her, so she sneaked out (her own words), went to a pay telephone and called.

Mrs. Collins answered, "Mrs. Collins, I'm calling from Bermuda, how are things going?"

"Oh, fine."

"And how's Danielle?"

"Oh, fine, she's right here. Here, I'll put her on. Danielle, it's your mother, come here and talk to her."

"Hello."

"Hi, Honey, it's Mother. How are you?"

"Oh, I'm fine, Mom, but I'm watching *Welcome Back Kotter*. I gotta go!"

PACKAGE DEAL

On the first day of school, the teacher had noticed Teddy's devastatingly deep blue eyes, but as time passed, they grew on her.

Finally one day she said to the six-year-old, "Teddy, where on earth did you get those beautiful blue eyes."

The boy grinned, then said, "They came with the face, Miss Gibbons!"

PAGING WEBSTER

Jennifer was just over two years of age. She had been playing with her next door friend when she came in the house crying her heart out.

Fearing she may have been hurt, her daddy rushed and picked her up. "What happened, Honey?" he asked. But the child was sobbing out of control and could not answer.

Dad observed no scratch or bruise, but she continued to cry. As she began to regain control, Daddy asked again, "What happened?"

"Marsha c –ca – ca – called me – a icky,—gookie,—piece o' gunk1"

"Well, now, Sweetie, that's all right, we don't care about that. We know you're a sweet little girl. You know you're our nice little sweetie; we don't care what Marsha calls us."

He continued to comfort her. The tears finally stopped flowing and she remained motionless on his lap. Finally she turned her head and looked up into the face of her big, strong, all-knowing protector.

"Daddy?"

"What Sweetie?"

"What's a icky, gookie, piece o'gunk?"

PARENT ABUSE

To say that Jeff at age nine and Paul at age seven, never did today what they could put off till tomorrow was probably to say that they were normal boys. Thus Mom found it necessary every once in a while—and this is probably to say that she was normal also—to crack the whip.

The boys had been especially lax since the onset of spring, so when it was time for the boys to be home from school, their mother phoned from work. Jeff answered.

"Jeff," she said, "you boys left the den in a real mess. Now you listen. I want you to clean up that den, make your beds and mow the lawn by the time I get home tonight. And believe me, it had better be done or you'll settle with your father!"

The response came quickly:

"Hey, lady, you've got the wrong number!"

Click!

PARENTAL EXAMPLE

Often an utterance is amusing only because it came from a child. You wouldn't give it a second thought if the following came from a lumberjack or a longshoreman, but understand that this tumbled out of the mouth of a three-year-old, and a female at that!

Grandma had cleaned out the car and when, while out shopping, the first few drops of rain hit the windshield, Kelley turned and looked in the back seat and then asked, "Grandma, where's my raincoat?"

"Oh, I took it in the house, Honey."

Whereupon came the response, "Jesus Christ, and here it is raining!"

PASS THE DRAMAMINE

Frankie had found a brightly colored caterpillar, had put it in a jar with a few twigs and leaves and brought it to school. The teacher was allowing him to take it around the room to show to the other children.

The bright colors fascinated the children but before they had all seen him, the caterpillar crawled beneath a leaf. Frankie shook the jar to try to force him back into view. Unsuccessful, he shook the jar even more vigorously until the teacher admonished him, "Oh, don't do that, the caterpillar won't like that."

"No," chimed in a little boy standing nearby, "how would you like it if you were in a jar and someone was shaking you all around? You could even make that caterpillar sick!"

"Wha'd you mean, sick?" Frankie snapped.

"Of course he could get sick, stupid, didn't you ever hear of jar sickness?"

PATENT NUMBER 1

Upon seeing a young man with well-groomed long hair and beard, Michael was overheard to say to his sister. "That looks like Jesus over there!"

"Who?" the little girl asked.

"Jesus," and then, cupping his hand aside his mouth, he whispered, "Jesus, you know, he's the one who invented Christmas!"

PENNIES FROM HEAVEN

Tracy and Steven were fighting over a penny found in Steven's room.

"It's mine," Steven said. "It was in my room."

"I know, but it's mine," Tracy insisted. "I lost it there."

The children's parents were quite sure the coin belonged to Steven, so they asked Tracy, "Well, if it's yours, where did you get it?"

"My teacher gave it to me."

"Your teacher gave it to you? What for?"

"She gave it to me for being good."

"She what? She gave it to you for being good?"

"Yes."

"I never heard of it. They don't give money in school for reasons like that."

"It's something new. They just started it."

"Well, I guess we'll have to telephone the teacher and ask her about it."

"You can't do that, she's a substitute teacher."

"Well, she'll have a phone at her home. What's her name?"

"I don't remember."

"Well, we'll call the principal. She'll know about the new policy of giving money to children for being good."

"You can't do that. The telephones up at the school aren't working."

"Well maybe they've got them fixed by now, we'll try and see." Mother went to the telephone, looked up the number and started to dial.

"Oh, I just remembered," Tracy said, "I found the penny on the playground at recess."

PERSONAL HIDEAWAY

Caroline enjoyed playing with Auntie Jean because the elder spent countless hours playing with the child.

On one occasion, the aunt reclined on the sofa and soon was dozing. Evidently desiring the participation of her aunt in some activity, yet reluctant to rouse her from her nap, the child tiptoed up close to the aunt and whispered, "Auntie Jean." The latter half-heard, yet remained in her semi-slumber. She was aware that the child moved away and became involved with her books and dolls, but soon she was back again.

This time, using her thumb and forefinger, the child parted her aunt's eyelids and again whispered, "Auntie Jean."

Amused and now fully awake, the aunt decided to feign sleep and observe the child's next move.

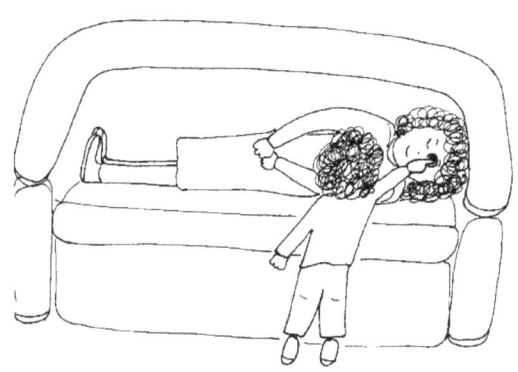

Again the child went back to her playthings, but shortly approached the sofa for the third time. Again with her thumb and forefinger, she parted the aunt's eyelids, this time much wider, saying,

"Auntie Jean, are you in there?"

PERSONAL PROPERTY

Juliana was three and it was her first day in Montessori School.

She had to go to the girls' room and when she was finished, the teacher asked, "Juliana, did you wash your hands?"

"No," the child replied.

"Well, you go back and wash your hands."

The child ignored the order and started to return to her regular activities.

"Juliana," the teacher said rather sternly, "you go back and wash your hands."

"Why?"

"Well, there are germs, you know."

Juliana put her hands on her hips and said as though disgusted with the teacher's ignorance, "Well, they're my germs!"

PHOTOGRAPHER'S CRIME

Little Connie was very fond of her Aunt Nelda, fond too, of Crandell to whom Nelda became engaged. Connie was flower girl at the wedding and heaped her affection on the couple as they departed on their honeymoon.

The newlyweds settled in a distant city, and business brought the groom back alone for a visit some three months after the wedding. Connie was thrilled at seeing him and clung to him constantly.

He showed pictures taken on the honeymoon, most of them at Grand Canyon. Connie was tucked in bed, but her door stood ajar and she overheard the adult conversation as they again more completely reviewed and chattered about the photographs.

Nightmares plagued Connie and her parents were up twice to calm and comfort her. The next morning the child looked worn; she was withdrawn and would have nothing whatsoever to do with her new uncle, and ran screaming to her mother when Crandell attempted to tease her out of her foul mood.

Finally her mother marched the child to her room and demanded to know the reason for her behavior. At first the girl would say nothing, but her mother was insistent.

"Uncle Crandell murdered Aunt Nelda!" the youngster blurted.

"What? Whatever makes you say such a thing?"

"I heard you say it yourself, Mommy and you can't lie to me just because I'm a little kid!"

"Say— say what? What did I say?"

"I heard it. I heard you say, 'You cut off the top of her head!'"

PLAN "A" ABORTED

Billy's Uncle Tom had come for a visit. The two had talked for a while, and when the novelty wore off, Billy went out to play. Subsequently the uncle and his sister, Billy's mother, engaged in conversation.

After a half-hour or so, Billy, age seven, came in whimpering. "Gee, Bruce and those other guys are nothing but bullies. They took my soccer ball and won't give it back. They push me around and everything."

Uncle Tom turned quickly to the boy and said. "I'll tell you what I'd do; I'd go out there and punch'em in the nose."

The lad turned and walked out the door.

"Oh, dear," Billy's mother said nervously, "those boys are big. I wonder."

She got up, Tom following, and went to the door. They saw Billy sitting on the front steps. The other boys were across the street in the school yard, kicking the soccer ball around. Yes, they were, indeed, big, husky boys. The two watched for a few minutes and it became evident that

Billy was not going to venture forth. They went back to the living room and their conversation.

In a few minutes they heard the door open and Billy appeared.

"Uncle Tom," he asked, "have you got any other ideas?"

PRECEDENT

"Jim," his mother commanded, "you go clean up the family room."

"Aw, gee, Mom, I promised the guys I'd meet 'em at four-thirty for softball."

"Well, it's just four now, you have plenty of time."

"No, I don't."

"Oh, come on, Jim, how long did it take you last time you cleaned the family room?"

"At least two hours."

"Oh, come now Jim, you weren't actually that long working on that room. You know that."

"Well yeah Mom, but you gotta remember I spend a lot of time fussing about it before I get down to business!"

PRE-MED

Nine-year-old Alana was eating a candy Easter egg and her aunt noticed a Band-Aid on her finger.

"Why are you wearing a Band-Aid?" the aunt asked.

"I cut my finger," the child answered. "I put the Band-Aid on to keep dirt out so the cut won't get infected. We're learning about that in school right now."

"How about all that candy you're eating?" the aunt asked. "Aren't you afraid that'll rot your teeth?"

"I don't know," was the response, "that's in chapter twelve and we're only on chapter eleven!"

PROBLEM IN DECIBELS

Shortly before the family reunion, Kellie's great grandmother had found a Mother Goose record made in the thirties or forties and decided to take it to the child. Kellie was thrilled with the story and carried the record around tightly held in her hand and tucked up under her arm.

She accosted everyone, insisting each person accompany her into the den where she would play the record. No aunt, no uncle, no cousin, not even the ones she had never known before, was exempt from her crusade. One by one they all gave in and submitted to the required listening.

But then there was Grandpa. Grandpa was going to be a problem. Kellie had noticed that when speaking to him, everyone got up close to his ear and spoke in a loud voice.

At what seemed the right moment, Kellie approached her grandfather, put her lips close to his ear and asked, "Grandpa, do you think your ears are loud enough to hear my record?"

PROPER, PROPER NAMES

Grandma had that trouble common to many grandparents: confusing the children's names. She was especially prone to call Kellie by the name of one of her other granddaughters.

Often she would address or refer to Kellie as Tiffany or Karen, then correct herself with "Kellie, I mean." This went on and on, to the extent, in fact, that Kellie more or less accepted the phrase as normal.

On one occasion, Grandma addressed the youngster as Tiffany and failed to correct herself, prompting Kellie to volunteer the necessary, saying, "You mean 'Kellie I mean.'"

PSALMS, CHAPTER 79, VERSE 13

The teacher announced that this week the class would be studying various forms of animal life and the factors distinguishing one classification from another.

In particular now, mammals were being discussed, and the teacher had explained that mammals differ from other animal forms in that they are warm-blooded and the young are fed by milk secreted by the female mammary glands.

After this explanation the teacher noted that dogs, cats, and, of course, cows, are mammals, then asked the members of the class to name others.

Hands quickly shot up, and there came the answers: "Horses." "Pigs." "Goats." "Sheep." "Elephants." "Wolves." "Foxes."

The teacher interjected that rodents are mammals also to which the students responded by mentioning rats and mice, and the teacher added squirrels, chipmunks and beavers.

Then the teacher asked for more examples, her purpose mainly being to see when someone would mention man.

"Kangaroo." "Giraffe." "Hippopotamus." "Bear." "Deer." "Moose." "Elk."

The recitation slowed as the children exhausted the list of the more common examples. "There is one, a very well-known one, one you all see every day," the teacher continued. "Surely you can think of it."

Quiet ensued. Then suddenly a hand went up. "Yes, Marilyn?" the teacher said.

"People." The child said.

"Right, Marilyn, right!" Then seeking to bring out once more the particular characteristics that identify mammals: warm blood and mother's milk, she asked, "And how is it we know that people are mammals?"

The child was quick and confident with her answer, "Because it says in the Bible that we are sheep!"

QUEST FOR BUSTARD'S ROOTS

Bustard was Julie's little brother. Julie was three years old. It was hard to know how old Bustard was because time didn't mean all that much to Julie, and Bustard existed entirely in Julie's imagination.

Now let's not misunderstand. None of this is to say that Bustard was not real. He was just about the most real thing in the whole world—to Julie!

For instance, when Dad brought tickets at the amusement park for Mom, himself and Julie, he'd jolly well better buy one for Bustard or there'd be trouble. (Of course, Dad had a system of deception to evade any unnecessary expense!) Anything that was purchased for Julie, had to be duplicated for Bustard, albeit that a simulation could be substituted for the real thing, but such simulation for sure had better be a material thing (maybe only a wad of paper) and better be referred to by the adults as reality.

Once when Julie was staying with Grandma, it suddenly became Bustard's birthday.

"Grandma, we have to go get Bustard a birthday present."

"Oh, I'm sorry, dear, but I don't have the car today. We have no way to get out and buy a present."

"Oh, but Bustard will feel so bad if he doesn't get a birthday present!" History does not record either the size or quantity of Bustard's tears, but no matter. Julie wept enough for the two of them!

The climax of Bustard's reality occurred in the super market checkout line a few weeks later. It was the cause of Julie's mother's cheeks turning a warm, rosy pink.

Julie was behind her mother in the line, and behind Julie stood a dignified appearing gentleman. Julie turned to the man and asked, "Are you Bustard's father?"

"No, who's Bustard?" the man asked.

"Oh, he's my little brother. I've been asking my mother who his daddy is, and she just can't remember!"

QUESTION FOR DAD

The Sunday school teacher was trying to get better acquainted with Diane who was three years old.

"Do you have any brothers or sisters?"

"No, I don't."

Then, mostly just to continue the conversation and perhaps a bit careless in her approach, the teacher asked, "Are you going to have any brothers or sisters?"

"I don't know; my daddy's been out to sea for almost a year, but just the minute he gets home, I'll ask him!"

QUICK RECOVERY

Jennifer and her older brothers were making a flower basket to give their mother as a surprise on Christmas morning. Grandma was overseeing the project and making suggestions. The boys had fallen into the habit of saying "Oh, God," whenever anything went wrong. Jennifer was picking up the habit, and Grandma finally decided it was time to call a halt.

"Now, listen, children," she said, "you don't use God's name that way. You use God's name when you're studying about him in Sunday School or when you're singing hymns or when you're praying, but you don't use it when something goes wrong or just as an expression. That's swearing and you mustn't do it."

The flower work continued and in the course of the project, Jennifer dropped a flower and it lost some petals.

"Oh, God," she exclaimed. Then suddenly realizing what she had said, and with a glance toward Grandma, she added quickly, and to the familiar tune, "is coming to town!"

QUIET DIET

My brother often tells this story in illustration of the observation that Canadians are much quieter than we in the States.

He was traveling by bus from Victoria to Nanaimo in British Columbia, and seated next to him was a boy he judged to be about seven years old.

The two visited, and my brother learned that the boy would be going on to Campbell River to visit his grandfather who would meet him at the bus station. Further pleasant conversation ensued, and my brother was impressed with the qualities of intelligence and politeness in the boy.

As the bus neared my brother's destination, he commented, "I'll be glad when we reach Nanaimo. I'm getting hungry."

The boy responded, "I'm getting hungry, too."

"Do you have anything to eat with you?" my brother asked.

"I have some potato chips."

"Oh, well then, you're all fixed."

"Oh, no, I can't eat them on the bus."

"Why not?"

"They're too noisy!"

QUITE POSSIBLY TRUE

It was parents' visiting day. It was also the day before election day, and the class had been studying about the political process.

The teacher was orally quizzing the class, but she was only calling on volunteers as she did not wish to embarrass any student in the presence of visitors.

Such questions as "Who is our Vice President?" "What is the job of our Secretary of State?" "How often do we elect a governor?" were met with upraised hands and answered correctly.

Then came the question, "What is a caucus?" There was a conspicuous pause but finally Terry's hand went up.

"Terry?" the teacher said.

The boy stood up, "A caucus is a dead body!"

RARE COINCIDENCE

Having the proper physical characteristics, Frank Duncan had been Santa Claus at the company Christmas party for several years.

Feeling certain that although his own daughter was now three, she would not recognize his voice amid all the magic and emotion of the Christmas aura, he consented again to be the jolly little old elf.

Santa would be giving a gift to everyone, but he would also be taking orders from the children for the big event now only a few days off. He took each child on his knee and visited a minute, asked what he or she would like for Christmas and then gave the child his gift.

There was a normal hubbub in the room but all became silent when Santa's own daughter climbed on his knee.

"Have you been a good little girl this year?"

"Well, I don't know."

"Oh, you don't know? Who would know?"

"My daddy."

"Does your daddy like you?"

"Yes."

"Do you like your daddy?"

"Yes."

"Is your daddy smart?"

"Yes."

"What makes you think your daddy's smart?"

"Cuz he has a ring just like yours!"

REACH FOR THE STARS

The Montessori teacher had taught the children a game called Magic 'Magination.

As an example, she asked them to close their eyes and imagine they were walking in a bowl of Jell-O; then they open their eyes and tell about their imagined experience.

On one occasion, she asked the children to close their eyes and imagine they were looking at a tree, the prettiest tree they had ever seen, their favorite tree. All of the children then described the tree that they had seen in terms of height, breadth, color, fruit, blooms, etc., all but Heidi.

"My tree," said Heidi, "was all covered with diamonds, beautiful, sparkling diamonds!"

The teacher asked, "Oh, my, how did the diamonds get on the tree?"

The question did not stump the child, no indeed. She replied, "I sprinkled them there during Magic 'Magination!"

REINCARNATION CONFIRMED

Pace was three and a half years old. Remember that.

Grandma came to visit and one morning she was busy in the kitchen. "Granma," Pace asked, "whatcha doin'?"

"I'm making cookies; grandmothers always make cookies for their grandchildren."

"What kind ja makin?"

"Oatmeal."

"How do you do that?"

"Oh, you mix a lot of stuff together and then you bake them in the oven for about fifteen minutes."

"What kind of stuff?"

"Oh, you use eggs, margarine, brown sugar, cinnamon, flour, nuts, raisins, all kinds of good stuff."

Pace wandered off. After a few minutes he returned with his teddy bear. "See," he said, lifting the teddy bear up so that he could see the procedure, "Grandma's making cookies." Then he seemed to be in thought for a moment and finally said:

"Ya know, Grandma, it's been seven years since I've had a really good oatmeal cookie!"

RELUCTANT POSTPONEMENT

Three-year-old Katie didn't like going shopping, but it was only going to be for a "couple of hours." However, the traffic was heavy and the stores were crowded. Mom couldn't find what she wanted in one mall, so they had to drive to another one.

It was hot. It was humid.

Katie began to whimper and complain. "I want to go home," she whined.

"It won't be much longer. Now you come along, stop whining, and be a good girl."

But the mood continued. When they got in the car to go do "just one more errand," Katie began to cry in earnest, not a tantrum, but just a good steady cry, more like a drizzle than a cloudburst.

"I tell you what," her mother offered, "if you stop crying, we'll go get some ice cream."

"Well, all—all—all right," the child agreed, but nevertheless, she continued her sobbing.

When they parked in front of the ice cream store, the mother said earnestly, "Now, Katie, you're going to have to stop that crying if you want any ice cream. We don't budge from this car as long as that crying is going on."

Katie reduced the cry back to a whimper and said, "Well, all right, if I have to stop crying to get the ice cream, I will, but as soon as I'm through with my ice cream, I'm going to start crying again!"

REQUEST FOR A FRONT ROW SEAT

Mom was frank in answering Stuart's questions about "where the baby was now."

He was satisfied that it was in her "tummy," and seemed confident that it would be safe there.

But as his mother grew bigger, there were more questions. She always answered them honestly although she sometimes skimped on the graphic details. "When it's time for the baby to be born, he'll come out into the world."

His next question was difficult, "Can I watch when he comes out the door?"

RESPECT FOR PROPERTY

Wanda had been to the library many times with her parents so she knew the procedure well. Now, however, at six years of age she stood before the librarian prepared to use her very own newly issued card to check out three books that she had selected with great care.

She was a bit nervous, yet she had a sense of having reached a milestone in her process of growing up—she could check out books all by herself!

The librarian took the books and the card, properly stamped the books and the library's record and handed the books and card back to the child. "Would you like to have a book marker?" she asked.

There was a bit of bewilderment and also embarrassment in the child's expression momentarily, then she replied, "Oh, no, I don't think so. My mother says I shouldn't mark in my books!"

REWARD FOR THE GOOD SAMARITAN

My friend, George, tells this story from his childhood. He emphasizes that all he knows of the event from his own remembrance is that: (1) It was a Saturday morning, and he was peddling his bike. Terry was sitting on the handle bars, and they were going to Cobbs Creek Park to play baseball. Each had a baseball glove hanging on his belt, and Terry was holding one end of a baseball bat while the other end dangled close to the rear of the bike's front wheel; and, (2) The kitten's pawing at the covers awakened him, and as he opened his eyes he became aware of something obstructing the vision of his left eye. Feeling the area with his hand, he realized that a bandage on his forehead extended down over his eye.

All that follows was told to George by others. He did not remember them, nor does he remember now, the events which occurred in the interval between the two above incidents.

A passing motorist saw the bat lodge between the wheel and the bike's frame. The bike seemed to simply collapse beneath the boys. George was thrown forward where his head struck a curb, and he bled profusely. Terry scrambled to his feet and ran away as fast as he could go.

The motorist lifted George, unconscious, onto the sidewalk and did his best to stem the flow of blood. He called to a passerby, asking him to summon the police.

The police arrived and applied further first aid. George seemingly regained consciousness. The police took the motorist and George to the police station.

Filling out a report, the police asked the man what happened, and he stated that he saw the dangling bat swing in between the wheel and frame causing the spill, saw George thrown head first into the curb and saw the other boy get up and run away.

Then the police questioned George. "Did this man hit you with his car?"

"Yes, he did."

Repeated questioning gleaned the same stories. Neither the motorist nor George contradicted himself, but they did definitely and directly contradict each other.

The motorist was held, and George's parents were called. George was taken to a hospital emergency room, examined, bandaged and taken home and put to bed where he fell asleep, later to be awakened by the kitten.

Meanwhile, the motorist remained in custody.

George's father phoned Terry's parents. They said Terry had come home with a broken tooth and badly shaken and had refused to utter a single word about the morning's events.

George's father went to Terry's home and pleaded with the boy to talk. He would not.

Finally the police were called; maybe the shock of being confronted by a uniformed officer would make the boy talk. It did. Terry confirmed the motorist's story in every detail. It was indeed the dangling bat that had caused the accident.

The accident had occurred before noon. The motorist was released at about four o'clock.

"I've wished a thousand times," says George, who is now in his sixties, "that I could find that good Samaritan who perhaps saved my life, so that I could apologize to him for all the grief I caused him when I was out of my head!"

RIGHT OUT OF BARNUM AND BAILEY

When Grandma arrived to stay a couple of weeks with her daughter and family who were spending the summer at the sea shore, she announced that she was anxious to get out and go fishing.

"Grandma," asked four-year-old Martin, "do you fish from a boat or from a pier?"

"Not either one," was the reply. "I prefer surf fishing."

It puzzled Grandma for a moment when the child responded with, "Re-e-e-ealy?" as his eyes widened, but she soon forgot the incident.

Next morning when the family was preparing to go fishing, Martin asked, "Grandma, is it alright if I bring my friend?"

"Fine with me, if it's okay with your mom and dad."

The boy went to the phone, dialed it and paused waiting for an answer, then:

"Hey, Tom, do you want to come and see my grandma fish from a surf board?"

ROAD SHOW

It was with some degree of pride that Chuckie brought home a five-foot bull snake and took it to his mother. The latter screamed bloody murder and ordered the boy to get the snake out of the house.

"Hey, Chuckie," the boy's Uncle Dewey chimed in, "put him in the garden. Bull snakes are good for gardens.'"

"Don't you dare," Mom said, "You take that slimy thing right back where you got it. It's not going in any garden of mine!"

"Aw, gee, Mom, it's a long way back there. I carried it all the way home 'cause I thought you'd like to see it."

"Okay, now I've seen it, you get it out of here. If it's so far, maybe your Uncle Dewey will drive you."

The pair got in the car, Chuckie in the back seat with the snake. As they drove, a sailor and two girls came toward them on their side of the road, walking.

"Show it to 'em, Chuckie," Dewey suggested.

After passing, Dewey glanced back. The girls were running like crazy down the ditch and the sailor was rolling on the ground holding his abdomen and laughing.

"What happened?" Dewey asked.

"Well, you said, 'throw it to 'em,' and I did!"

ROMANCE FROM AFAR

Wilma was shopping with her mother, and they were in the fruit department.

The child fingered some oranges, held one up to her mother, saying, "How about some of these, Mommy?"

"Well, no, I think these look better over here, these Sun-Kist."

Shopping was concluded, and on the way home, the child said, "Mommy, I have a question."

"Yes?"

"How does the sun get down to the ground so it can kiss an orange?"

RUBE GOLDBERG REBORN

The family was gathered on a hot and humid Sunday afternoon. Evening was approaching and the insects which had been bothersome all day were getting worse, precipitating a discussion about the pests and ways of thwarting them.

"Poor Ginger," Craig's father said to his brother, speaking of the family's Springer Spaniel. "I wish I knew some way to get rid of those fleas."

The dog was intermittently scratching, then biting here and there on his body, obviously annoyed no end by the pests.

Now Craig's mother claims that she can always tell when Craig is in deep thought. His brow, she says, will take on deep furrows, all slanting down toward his nose. He becomes silent and completely detached from anything going on around him. When he is in such deep thought, she always knows that he is working on a problem, and a solution will soon be forthcoming. The solution may be practical and it may not, probably the latter, but it will always be interesting.

The insects won the battle and the adults got up and went inside. The conversation about the heat, humidity and pests had run its course, and the adults were now talking about interest rates.

Craig remained in his trance on the lawn chair.

Finally, the lad came in the house and joined the others. The furrows were gone from his brow and he spoke cheerfully and with confidence: "I've figured out how it can be done," he said.

"How what can be done, Son?" his father asked.

Mom recognized the sign; she knew they were about to have the benefit of a great mental effort.

"How we can get rid of Ginger's fleas," the lad said, answering his father.

"Good, and how will we do that?" Dad asked.

"Well, we'll go down to the lake. We'll get a piece of moss, oh, about as big as your hand. We'll put it on Ginger's back and send him for a swim. The fleas won't want to get drowned so they'll crawl up on Ginger to get out of the water. When they get to his back, he'll feel 'em all up there and he'll know they went there to get out of the water. When he knows this, he'll go deeper in the water and the fleas will all get up on the piece of moss. When he knows they're all on the moss, he'll go completely under water, and the moss will float away, and Ginger won't have fleas anymore!"

RUDE AWAKENING

It was traditional that sometime during the holidays, Dad took each of the three children to his club for lunch. He took them separately, purposely emphasizing the one-on-one, father-child relationship, making the event very special for each child.

Craig and Martha had each had their turn, and the comments about the elegance of the event—the club, the food—flew thick and fast around the house.

Tomorrow was Beth's turn. Anticipation of the event consumed the child's every moment. She hardly ate dinner that night and went to bed early, evidently thinking this would hasten the coming of the eventful day.

While her brother was getting ready for bed, he made a noise that awakened the child and she began to cry.

Her mother went to her door. The cry was not a frightened cry, nor was it a sobbing; it was more of an "I dropped my sucker in the mud" cry.

"Darling, what's the matter?" her mother asked, entering the room. "Did you have a bad dream?"

"No, I didn't. I had a good dream."

"Well then, why are you crying? There's nothing to cry about in a good dream."

"Oh, yes, there is. I was dreaming I went to daddy's club, and the waiter brought me a big dish of ice cream with strawberries on it, and then that darn Craig woke me up before I even had a chance to taste it."

SAFELY ATTIRED

Claude was questioning his grandfather. "Grandpa," he asked, "why don't you have any hair on the top of your head?"

"Oh, many men lose their hair; it's called baldness. When you get to be my age, you'll probably lose yours too because at least to some degree it's hereditary."

"What does that mean?"

"Hereditary means that it's passed on from one generation to another—from father to son, to son and so on."

"How does that happen?"

Grandfather knew he was getting in over the boy's head, but he also realized he was getting in a bit over his own when he said, "Well, it's in your genes."

"Then I don't have to worry," the boy remarked, "'cause I don't wear jeans!"

SCARLET LETTER

It was customary in the Congregational Church for the minister to tell a children's story, following which and prior to the sermon the little ones exited to pursue other activities. On special days, the minister tied the children's story time into the theme of the event.

Today was Mother's Day and the minister asked, "Who was the first mother?"

A hand shot up.

"Eve," came the reply.

"And who was the mother of our Lord."

"Mary," came the prompt response.

"Now which one of the Ten Commandments do we think of when we think of our mothers?"

Silence ensued for several seconds

"Which one of the Ten Commandments reminds us of our mother?" came the rephrased question.

Now a hand went up, and the minister nodded, recognizing a small boy sitting with his mother who was divorced.

Came the answer: "Thou shall not commit adultery!"

SECRET ENTRANCE

The family had attended church, then had dinner downtown, and now was walking leisurely along the avenue window shopping.

Three-year-old Gary was fascinated by something in a store window and said, "Let's go in here."

"We can't, Honey, the stores are closed," his mother said.

"No, this one isn't."

"Yes, it is. This is Sunday."

"But this store's open."

"No, it isn't."

"Well then, how'd that fly get in there?"

SEEKING THE HIGHEST BIDDER

Jennifer had lost a tooth. There was considerable talk about placing it under her pillow in anticipation of the tooth fairy.

"Mom," asked Mike, Jennifer's older brother, "can I be the tooth fairy? Can I put the money under her pillow and take the tooth after she goes to sleep?"

"You mean with your own money?" his mother teased.

But Mike took her seriously, "Sure, I'll do it with my own money."

"Well, okay, of course you can if you want."

Nine o'clock came; Jennifer was put to bed, and a short while later Mike switched a dime for the tooth.

"Gee, that tooth fairy is sure getting stingy," Jennifer commented the next day. "She only left a dime. She always left a quarter before."

Three days passed.

When the children arrived home from school, their mother announced. "Guess what, Grandma and Grandpa are coming for Thanksgiving. They'll stay a week and they'll be here Saturday."

When the children were alone, Jennifer said, "Mike I want my tooth back. Get my tooth and give it to me."

"I don't have your tooth. How can I give it back?"

"Oh, yes, you do. You took it."

"Of course I didn't take it. The tooth fairy took it. You know that."

"Oh, you know very well there's no such thing as a tooth fairy, and besides I know you took it. I wasn't even asleep."

"Well, how about my dime?" Mike asked.

"Okay, cheap skate, you can have your silly dime back."

"So why do you want your dumb tooth back anyway?"

"'Cuz Grandpa's coming, and I know—he's got lots of money!"

SERIOUS OVERSIGHT

Dad had just picked up Heather at Sunday School and was heading home. As he was preparing to overtake a slow-moving car ahead of him, it swerved toward his path.

"Good Lord!" he said as he hit the brakes.

He followed behind the car for a block or two. It continued to swerve slightly but was slowing all the time, till finally the father thought it safe to pass. As he started around, he gave a brief toot on his horn, but then the car ahead veered even more violently than before, causing him to brake sharply and swerve over against the left hand curb.

"Gee-zuss Christ!" he swore.

Heather seemed distraught for a moment, but when she realized an accident had been avoided and regained her composure, she came forth with a reminder:

"Don't forget the baby, Moses, Daddy!"

SEX DISCRIMINATION

The hassle of getting seven-year-old Scott to wash his hands was a never ending problem in the Glann family. Alternately, Mom would simply give up, but, at other times, would apply various restrictions to get him to remember to wash.

Scott's sisters, Debbie, eleven, and Diana, nine, were having a slumber party, the main feature of which was a taffy-pull. Including the sisters, there were eight girls present.

Scott had been out but came in as the girls were pulling the candy. He asked his mother if he could pull taffy too. The girls protested—this was a *girl's* party, but their mother said, "Now Scott is a member of this family and whatever goes on in this house, he can be a part of it."

Mother was busy and consequently failed to notice when Scott took a portion of the goo and started pulling it.

Naturally, there was a lot of chatter, laughing and confusion with ten people in the kitchen. Suddenly Diana's face turned sober.

"Mom," she said accusingly, "how come all us girls got white taffy and Scott got gray?"

SHARE THE JOY, SHARE THE PAIN

It was due to a sledding accident that five-year-old Mark had to have two front teeth pulled. As yet, neither he nor his older brother was aware of the tooth fairy since up to this time, neither had lost any teeth. Now their mother was telling Mark about the treasure that might appear under his pillow if he would stop fussing immediately and place the teeth under his pillow when he went to bed.

Miraculously, the gum stopped hurting and Mark brightened up.

"Really, Mom? How much money does the fairy leave?"

"Oh, different amounts, it varies according to whether you've been good, your attitude about losing your tooth, how you've behaved at the dentist, and so forth."

Stuart, two years Mark's senior, had taken all this in and posed the question, "Won't Mark have to give me half the money since you've always said we should share?"

"Well, you'll be losing some teeth before long. You'll get your turn. The tooth fairy will still be around when you need him."

"But that's not fair. You've always told us we must share."

"Yeah," Mark put in, "but you weren't asking to share when I was sitting there in the dentist's chair and he was pulling my teeth!"

SHORT CUT

Sliding down the banister was forbidden, but when Larry, at age eight, had been excused from class to go to the boys' room, he thought he was alone in the halls so he broke the rules and took a quick slide to the floor below. There, he found he was, not only not alone, but indeed, was face to face with the school principal who had just come around a corner.

Aghast, the principal realized that if he had fallen forward he might have tumbled down the stairs but if he had fallen backwards, it was possible he could have plunged two stories.

She went swiftly to the boy and took him firmly by the shoulders. "Young man," she asked, "do you realize where you'd go if you'd fallen backwards off that banister?"

"Yes, ma'am," he replied politely, "I'd go to heaven!"

SHORT SHORTCAKE

Jake's aunt had come to visit and brought a whole gallon of plump, luscious strawberries.

"Jake," his mother said, "I want you to run to the store and get a Sara Lee pound cake for dinner."

Returning, the child put the cake in the refrigerator and his mother went on with preparations for dinner.

Only when the main course was over and Mother began preparing the dessert did she discover to her amazement that the cake was chocolate.

"Jake," she called, "I distinctly told you to get a pound cake! What's the matter with you anyway?"

"I know, Mom, but I looked at every cake in the store, and they just didn't have any. The closest I could come was that fourteen-ounce one!"

SILENT CONFESSION

Henry, age nine, Nell, seven, and Jamie, six, were left with the housekeeper for two days while their mother and father made a trip out of town.

It was in the late 1800s, before modern affluence had led children to expect the material and more expensive gifts common today.

When Mama and Papa returned from their trip, Papa produced three apples of varying sizes and set them on the table.

He then announced that the housekeeper was to state which child had been the best behaved and that that child was to have the largest apple, that the housekeeper was then to state which child had been the next best behaved, and that—

He had proceeded only that far in his announcement when Jamie promptly stepped forward and took the smallest apple!

SIMPLE MATTER OF TASTE

Little Benny, age five, had overheard his mother's answer to his older brother's query of, "Hey, mom, what's for dinner?"

"We're having that leftover ham, au gratin potatoes, squash and Jell-O salad."

When Benny came to the table it was without enthusiasm. He picked away at his food for a while—the meat, the squash, then the salad. He eyed the others curiously as they ate. He noticed they did so with the usual gusto. Finally he tried a tiny bite of the potatoes; then soon he was eating with his usual zest and resumed his normal demeanor.

"Gee, Mom," he said, "I don't think these potatoes taste rotten!"

SNAP COURSE

Claudia had attended Montessori School where it is the practice for the child to initiate appropriate work and the teacher oversees, directing only when necessary.

Now, the child was in public school but came back one day to visit her former school mistress.

"Claudia," the latter asked, "how do you like going to Hoover School?"

"Well, really, it's kind of dumb," the child replied. "The teacher does all the work and all we do is just sit there!"

SOME THINGS NEVER CHANGE!

In July, eight-year-old Laura had gone from Wisconsin to visit her grandmother in Georgia. Grandma thought the child should be exposed to some of the Southern grandeur so arranged to take a tour which would include some of the historic spots.

It was already very hot and humid when the pair boarded the bus for the all-day tour. By two p.m., Laura had grown weary, but the main feature was still to come.

The bus turned into a long lane, beneath huge live oak trees which spread out to make a veritable tunnel through which the vehicle passed. This led to a magnificent old plantation, a huge white mansion with massive colonnades which supported the roof over a wide veranda.

They toured the house as the guide explained in eloquent terms the lavish life style of the early plantation owners in years long gone. On the rear veranda, the guide again waxed eloquent, "Here, in those golden days," he explained, "one could stand and look out across the lush cotton fields and hear the plaintive melodies as the workers sang old southern tunes to lessen the boredom of their toil."

As the crowd turned and started filing back into the house, Grandma lingered, still gazing out across the vast field. "Oh, Laura," she said, "Can't you just imagine, can't you just feel how it must have been in those days?"

"Yeah," the child responded, "I sure can—hot and humid!"

S. P. C. A. CENSORSHIP

At age eight, Bruce watched the evening news along with his parents with a sort of half-detached attitude. Some items interested him and held his attention; others he ignored.

During the Vietnam conflict, the news constantly showed scenes of battle areas and reported on the guerrilla warfare. Bruce showed little interest in the war at first, but after weeks and weeks of the news media drumming on the same subject, he settled down and watched the war news intently.

Finally, he said to his parents, "Gee, the news is always talking about gorilla warfare. Where do they get all those gorillas, and why do they always talk about them but never show them on TV?"

STAR WARS

Mary had attended a program at the planetarium with her parents.

Silent films with simulations of all sorts of heavenly phenomena were shown, with a lecturer supplying descriptions and explanations. Most fantastic, at least to Mary, were stellar explosions, and the speaker explained that because of the extreme distance from the earth that these explosions occur, it could sometimes take millions of years for the visual evidence of them to reach the earth.

Mary's apprehensions about the material she had been seeing and hearing on the six-thirty news surfaced as the family was driving home from the planetarium.

"Daddy, those explosions," she asked, "are they ours or the Russians'?"

STATE OF THE ART EATERY

When Diana was three, a baby brother came into the family. The mother had some problems and was unable to nurse the newcomer. Thus, Diana had no occasion to see an infant fed by natural means.

The family had a cat named Rachael, and, cats being cats, she produced a litter of four kittens.

When Diana observed the young taking sustenance, she ran to her mother saying "Mommy, Mommy, the kittens are all chewing Rachael."

"Oh, Honey, that's all right, that's natural," her mother was quick to assure her. "That's the way the babies get their milk."

A few days later, Diana was showing the kittens to a friend. "Look, they're all different colors. They don't even have their eyes open yet, and look here on Rachael's tummy. See these," she said putting her finger on a nipple, "these are the bottles!"

STICK WITH THE SUBJECT, DAD

"In the spring, a young man's fancy often turns to thoughts of love." Well, maybe so, but the thoughts of millions of others are turning to seed catalogs.

Elexia, at the age of nine, had sent for the L.L. Bean catalog. She loved the pictures which brought dreams of the lush summer. But sooner or later, Dad customarily examined the catalog with more practical objectives in mind. He would need to order radish, pea, bean, carrot, lettuce and other seeds.

He went to Elexia's room where she was deep in home work. "Elexia," he said, "let me take your L.L. Bean catalog for a while."

"Okay, Daddy," the child said, handing him the catalog, "but don't forget to bring it back."

Dad left but didn't reply.

"Daddy," Elexia called, "did you hear me? I said don't forget to bring it back."

Dad turned around and said, "Elexia, what do you mean, 'don't forget to bring it back?' I'm your *daddy*! Remember?"

"Okay Daddy, I know, I know, but we're not talking love right now; we're talking seed catalog. Gosh!"

STRAIGHTFORWARD ANSWER

Grandfather hadn't seen Sandra since she was four, and when he came to visit when she was nine, he was pleased to see that she was a well-adjusted and advanced child.

The two hit it off immediately, and Sandra took great delight in showing him her room and all the goodies in it.

Grandfather thought it would be a good idea if he took an interest in her school work so he asked her what she was studying. She recited her subjects and this led to her bringing out some homework and asking him to quiz her.

There were some questions on geography and as he asked them, she banged right back with the answers.

"My goodness," he said, "you certainly know your geography, don't you?"

"Yes, I do," she said. "Now here are my arithmetic questions. Ask me those."

Again she zipped right through, answering every question quickly and accurately.

"My goodness, you are a precocious young lady, aren't you?"

"Yes, I am."

"Do you know what precocious means?"

"Yes, it means that I'm smarter than you are!"

STRANGE DIET

It is doubtful as to whether or not the many worries mothers have regarding their children's appetites are justified. Nevertheless, many find it difficult not to be concerned when their child eats like a canary.

Barry's mother, when trying to force more food down the youngster, exclaimed in exasperation. "My land, you don't eat as much as your baby sister; what on earth do you live on?"

Quick and to the point came the answer: "I live on Elm Street!"

STRONG UNION

Kelly looked forward with great anticipation to the fulfillment of his airline pilot father's promise to show him through the cockpit of a jetliner.

The questions came fast and furiously, but, the skilled father answered them forthrightly.

"What are all these clocks for?"

"Those aren't clocks," the father replied, then went on to explain in as simple language as possible the functions of the various dials and instruments.

"Where do you sit?"

"Here, like this," the father answered, taking his seat, fastening his seat belt, and putting on the head phones.

"What makes the plane go off the ground?"

"When this dial shows we're going fast enough, I pull back on this wheel; that changes the slant of the wings and up we go."

"What's this?" the child asked, fingering a switch panel.

"That's the automatic pilot."

"What's an automatic pilot?"

"That's what flies the plane; when we get up, we just set the automatic pilot, like this," he continued, demonstrating, "and it flies the plane."

"Do the people at United know you let that thing fly the airplane?"

"Of course."

The child's expression was a mixture of surprise and confusion. "Well, gee," he asked, "if that thing does all the work, how come they pay you all that money?"

SUCCINCT EVALUATION

Jeffery, age three, was being exasperatingly silly. Well, on second thought, he was really rather cute. It was only exasperating because of the press of time.

The family was preparing for Sunday School and church and Jeffery insisted on goofing off—giggling—gibbering—ignoring his parents' commands, then mocking them, ever amid more giggling.

As time grew shorter, his mother finally grabbed him firmly by the shoulders, shook him slightly and said, "Jeffery, Jeffery Cole, you settle down now and listen to me."

The child's face became serious and he looked his mother straight in the eye.

"Now, Jeffery, there is a time to be silly and there is a time to be nice."

They stood there facing each other directly, the child's face still dead serious but registering no reaction to his mother's statement.

Finally, as though having given his mother's remark due and serious consideration, he said,

"Actually, that's dumb!"

SUNSHINE STATE

One day while fishing with his son and family, Grandfather discovered that he had forgotten the protective lotion that normally he puts on his nose which was inclined to become unusually rosy if exposed to the hot sun too long, so he slid a small piece of brown paper under his glasses that extended down over his nose.

Summer passed, autumn too, and in December a letter came from Grandpa stating that he and Grandma were going to the Florida Keys for a couple of months. This letter was read at the dinner table. Jim, age seven, was silent for a long while, then: "Gee, I wouldn't think Grandpa would want to go to Florida."

Curious, his father asked, "Why?"

"'Cuz gee, he looks awfully silly with that dumb paper on his nose!"

SUPREME TATTLETALE

Debbie, when in her thirties, told this story on herself.

When she was five her hair was black, very thick, very coarse. She lived with her father who was all thumbs when it came to "fixing" a girl's hair, so he delegated the job to his sister, Debbie's Aunt Martha.

Gentleness was not one of Martha's outstanding traits, and she did the hair up in braids so as to reduce the frequency of the chore.

She pulled the braids tight and the child found no pleasure whatsoever in the ordeal. In plain English, it hurt! The course Debbie decided to take makes no sense to an older mind. The child reasoned only that: no hair, no braiding; no braiding, no hurt. Other consequences were not considered, could not occur.

She got the scissors and cut all her hair to a length of about a half inch. She did it all by feel, didn't think about using a mirror. Now she had the hair there in her hands and on the vanity. She could see it. She reasoned one step further. If she could see it, her father could see it. Dad wouldn't like the idea. Therefore, dispose of the hair.

Vividly she recalls placing neatly a layer of papers in the trash container, then in orderly fashion laying all the hair—every strand—on the paper, then thoroughly covering it with more paper, neatly tucking it down so that not one hair could possibly be seen.

Mission accomplished.

Dad came home.

Dad exploded!

"You crazy, dumb kid! Whatever got into your nutty head to cause you to do such a stupid thing?"

"But," says Debbie, now, "I couldn't figure what had gone wrong. Every hair was totally covered up, undisturbed, out of sight. I assumed that Dad could only see what I could see. I, of course, I couldn't see my shorn head. It simply never occurred to me that he could. I was positive that he could not have seen the discarded hair. How then…?"

Ah, suddenly it was all so obvious! How could I have overlooked a factor so basic? I raised my eyes skyward.

"God," I said, "why did you tell him?"

SURPRISE PARTY

The preschoolers were going on a field trip, visiting a farm on the outskirts of town.

The corn was just barely peeping through the black earth. The group looked out over the open field and the farmer told the children about the planting, the growing season and the harvesting. Then it was on to the out buildings and the animals, which, of course interested the children most.

Their host showed them the chickens and ducks, the hogs, the horses, sheep and goats, pausing as he went on to say a few words about each species, their habits, diet, etc. He then led them to the cow barn where he knew the cows would be lined up at their stanchions eating hay.

He threw open the door, and there before the children stood the chewing cows.

"Oh look, Miss Stevens," said one little girl to her teacher, "a party!"

SURVIVAL

A friend witnessed this scene in a super market.

A mother was pushing her two little boys in a shopping cart. Each time the cart came within reaching distance of a shelf, the older boy grabbed some item from it, either for close inspection or to place in the cart. Following the example of his brother, the younger boy started doing likewise.

In a patient and rather casual manner, the mother placed the items back on the shelves, sometimes having to wrest them from a tightly clenched little fist.

Soon the mother, tired of the repeated performances, admonished the children to desist. But, you know children and soft-voiced admonishments, just as you know water on a duck's back.

But finally mother awoke fully to the fact that her easy going approach to the problem was not getting the job done. She suddenly grabbed the boys by the shoulders, turned them to face her, and said, "Now you two listen to me! I'm going to find me two little boys and I'm going to knock their heads in!"

The younger boy froze, his face deadly serious, his gaze fixed on his mother's harsh countenance. The older boy looked briefly at his mother with the same expression, then he immediately looked away, slowly turning his head as he surveyed the entire store. Then he suddenly stretched out his arm and pointed, saying,

"Look, Mom, there are two little boys right over there!"

TEAM WORK

Julie was two when she stayed a while with her grandmother.

One day the elder was vacuuming. Julie pulled the electric cord out of the wall socket, giggled and then ran and hid.

Grandma chuckled to herself, patiently plugged the cord back in and continued her vacuuming.

Again the child slipped into the room and repeated her previous performance, and again Grandma laughed and continued her work.

The child's excitement escalated. She giggled louder, toddled faster, and her demeanor became more animated when she pulled the plug the third time. Her exuberance became ever more intense and Grandma's began to wane.

The fourth time, Grandma decided she must put a stop to the horseplay if she was ever to finish the vacuuming. She sought out the child and took her by the shoulders. "Now, listen, Honey, I'm trying to get my work done. When you played the trick the first time, it was cute, but you've got to stop it now and let me finish."

The child heard, but the spark in her eye was not erased.

"Hey, Gramma," she said, still giggling, "I not cop-er-ate, does I!"

THAT'S A HARD, COLD WORLD OUT THERE

Libby was only two and very tiny. She was starting Montessori school and her mother emphasized that this was a very important part of growing up. The child walked happily into the school room, no fears, no hesitation, no qualms. When her mother left her, she hardly noticed.

She entered into all the routines with enthusiasm and enjoyed every minute. That night she bubbled over telling Mom and Dad all about the experience.

But after a few days, the novelty wore off and she began to miss her mother.

When her mother picked her up at the end of the fourth day, the child said, "Mommy, I don't think I like school, I don't want to go back anymore."

"Oh, but, Honey, you must go, don't you remember I told you, school is a very important part of growing up."

"I know, Mommy, but I've decided I don't want to grow up. From now on I'm growing down!"

THE BIG ONE THAT GOT AWAY

Jimmy, age four, had been in bed for a quarter hour when his parents suddenly heard crying and his mother went to his room and asked, "What's the matter, Jimmy?" Between sobs he was able to say, "A big fish is coming to get me!"

"Oh, now, Honey, you just had a bad dream. There's no fish, you turn over and go back to sleep. You'll be all right."

"No, I didn't dream it. I haven't even been asleep yet."

She turned on the light so that the child would come fully awake and see that he was in his own room. With a hug she settled him back in the bed, turned out the light, closed the door and left.

But in a few minutes there was a repeat performance, the big fish was coming to get him. This time he was even more convinced, and it took longer to settle him.

And then again in only two or three minutes, there was a third act. This time the cry bordered on hysteria. It was the same problem, the big fish. When his mother could not settle him, she called his father. She had, of course, given the father a blow by blow, but he didn't let on that he knew the problem and so, as Mother slipped out of the room, he made a new beginning. "Jimmy, what is the trouble?" he asked.

"There's a b – b – big f – f—fish com – com – coming to get me!"

"A big fish?"

"Yes, and he – he – he's coming to get me!"

"How big is the fish?"

"He's jus – jus – just big."

"Is he this big?" the father asked, placing his hands about two feet apart.

"Bigger."

"This big?" the father asked, stretching his hands as far as possible.

"Bigger than that."

"Oh boy, I've never even seen a fish that big. I'd sure like to see him. When he comes will you promise to call me so I can see him?"

"Yes."

The father slowly and gently lowered the now quieted child into his bed, all the time "oohing" and "aahing" about the size of the fish and repeating that he wouldn't want to miss seeing him.

"Now you promise to call me when the fish comes, because I sure want to see him. I'll leave the door ajar because I don't want to miss hearing when you call."

In two or three minutes the father tiptoed to the door.

"Jimmy, has the fish come yet?"

"No, not yet."

Three or four minutes passed.

"Jimmy, has the fish come yet?"

Faintly, "No."

A few minutes later. "Jimmy, has the fish come yet?" Complete silence. End of problem. End of story.

THE DIET DECADE

"Mommy," Jimmy asked, "what is that Daddy said his grandpa is?"

"I guess I don't know what you mean. I don't know what you're talking about."

"Oh, it was an octa—, an octa—something."

"Oh, yes, he said his grandpa is an octogenarian."

"What's that?"

"That's a person that is eighty years old or in his eighties. Octa means eight. Septi means seven and a septuagenarian would be in his seventies. Sexa refers to six; a sexagenarian is in his sixties."

Jimmy seemed satisfied with the answer.

Jimmy's best friend was Sammy and a few days later Jimmy asked his mother, "Mom, how old is Sammy's grandmother."

"I haven't the slightest idea, Honey, why?"

"Well, Sammy says she's a vegetarian!"

THE GIFTED GIFT

Grandma had acquired the habit of referring to Teddy as "my darling little grandson," which, no question, he was.

On his eighth birthday she gave him one of the newfangled watches – the kind that has all sorts of buttons and can provide all sorts of useful and not-so-useful information. The child did not immediately master all the functions and, before the day was over, seemed a bit frustrated in his efforts to do so. When, in the evening, Grandma departed for home, he thanked her for the watch but there wasn't much enthusiasm in his appreciation.

He let the watch lay for a few days, but then began working with it again and before long he could produce the time in any of the twenty-four time zones around the world.

Considering this a fantastic accomplishment, he enthusiastically phoned his grandmother. "Grandma," he said excitedly, "I learned how to work my watch. I can do anything with it. I can tell you what time it is in Russia or Africa or anywhere. I can make it be tomorrow or I can make it be yesterday. You just tell me what you want and I can do it!"

Grandma chuckled. "Well, my goodness," she said, "if you can do all that with your watch, I guess I'd like to have you turn it back about forty years and make me a girl again."

"Aw, gee, Grandma," came the reply, "you wouldn't want me to do that. If I did that, you wouldn't have any darling little grandson anymore!"

THE NEW NEW MATH

Sharon didn't seem to be interested in numbers. She knew she was five years old. She knew she had seven dolls. She knew she lived at Four Cromwell Lane. She knew her phone number was 353-7001. She knew her bedtime was nine o'clock, sometimes ten, so who should care about numbers up in the thirties or seventies or hundreds?

She could count to ten, but there it ended. Her parents had tried to teach her that above nine and into the teens, it was simply a matter of putting a one in front of the other digits, from zero to nine. Then for the twenties, you simply put a two before the other digits. Then the thirties and higher numbers, likewise.

When finally a note came from the teacher stating that Sharon seemed to be a bright girl but she was having trouble with numbers, her father sat her down and lectured: "Now you listen, young lady, there's no reason in the world for you not to learn your numbers. There's to be no TV for you until you can count to one hundred, and when I get home Friday night if you can't count to a hundred there'll be more restrictions, is that understood?"

"Yes, Daddy."

On Wednesday when the child came home she promptly turned on the TV.

Her mother confronted her, "Sharon, what are you doing watching TV? Have you learned your numbers? If not your daddy will be furious!"

"Yes, I've learned them. I can count to one hundred."

"Let me hear you do it."

"Nope," the child said, with a spark of defiance and triumph in her eyes. "I'm going to save it for Daddy. He's the one who made me learn it!"

Her manner was convincing so her mother did not press for a recital. She only said, "Well, alright, but I warn you, you know your daddy means what he says, and you'd better be prepared to perform when he gets home."

Sharon's father arrived home late Friday. Dinner had been held for him, and while the family ate, the events of his trip were discussed.

As ten o'clock approached, Dad said, "Bedtime, Sharon, better get on the move."

"Daddy," the child asked, "haven't you forgotten something?"

"No, Sweetie, I haven't. The numbers I haven't forgotten. We'll go into that in the morning."

"I want to do it now."

"Why now, why not tomorrow, why the rush?"

"Because after I count to one hundred, I have a surprise for you!"

"Okay, start counting."

The child was sitting on a straight chair, her legs hanging loosely, and as she began to count, she swung her legs alternately in rhythm with her count, "one, two, three—nine, ten, eleven—nineteen, twenty, twenty-one—forty-six, forty-seven," everything going nicely, legs swinging vigorously, reflecting confidence, "seventy-nine, eighty, eighty-one," and finally, "ninety-eight, ninety-nine, *one hundred!*"

"Hurray!" Dad exclaimed as both he and Mom applauded. "See, that wasn't difficult. We knew you'd find it easy if you just settled down to business."

The legs continued to swing. "And now are you ready for the surprise?"

"Sure, ready, what's the surprise?"

"Nobody had to help me with this. I figured it out all by myself, I can count on up from one hundred."

"Oh, great, that's wonderful. Let's hear you do it."

The legs began swinging even more violently, this was Sharon's hour of triumph—what she'd been looking forward to ever since Wednesday. She counted: "One hundred and one, two hundred and two, three hundred and three, four hundred and four, five hundred and——!"

THOU SHALT NOT, BUT THEY DID

Mark, John, Bill, and Kevin, all between the ages of seven and nine, more than once had been forbidden by their parents ever to go on the levy along the Mississippi river. Trains sped along the tracks atop the levy at a dangerous clip and the boys were too young to realize the hazard.

They were too young, also, to always mind their parents. One day they ventured forth on their bicycles into the forbidden territory, bumping along from tie to tie. They alighted from their bikes to search for coal balls to use as slingshot ammunition.

As they became absorbed in their quest, they wandered farther and farther down the tracks and were oblivious to a far off whistle. But they became alert when they heard a deep rumble. They looked back up the track toward their bikes. Within the parallel rails, they saw a tiny but bright light. They broke into a run, toward the oncoming light which now loomed ominously in the square black center of the front of a thundering locomotive.

When the boys were still a hundred yards from the bikes, it became obvious that the race was lost, and they plunged down the embankment of the levy into the dense brush that bordered it.

There, four disobedient boys watched as four bicycles were ground to rubble.

TIME MARCHES ON

Teaching twenty-seven years in one classroom may be something of a record, but still this could be accomplished without too much gray hair or too many wrinkles, and, as a matter of fact, Miss White thought she was pretty well preserved. She was not yet fifty, almost perhaps, but not quite.

A young child does lack some perspective in these matters, and it was thus that little Freddie Walker asked Miss White, "Did you have Ned Walker in school?"

The teacher paused to think. It was a very small school, and even if she hadn't personally taught him, she thought she should probably know him, but the name rang no bell.

"No, Freddie," she replied, "I don't believe I did, why, is he your brother?"

"Oh, no, he's my grandfather!"

TONGUE ON CHEEK

Bea had been eating chocolate, the evidence of which spread from nose to chin and almost from ear to ear.

Grandma got a wash cloth, dampened it, and approached the child.

"No, Grandma, no," she protested, squirming to elude her. "I'm not done licking yet!"

TOO FAST-TALKING TEACHER

Cheryl had mastered kindergarten, but when she went into first grade, she had a different teacher and she was having problems.

When she was queried by her parents, she often didn't have the answers, and seemed frustrated.

A parent-teacher conference disclosed that Cheryl sometimes seemed slow to understand.

"Cheryl," her father asked on the evening after the conference, "Your teacher tells us you're having trouble in school. What seems to be the problem?"

"I don't know."

"She says that sometimes she'll explain something, and then you don't seem to know what she's said. Don't you pay attention when she's talking?"

"Yes, I do, but it just seems like I can't listen fast enough!"

TOP BILLING

It was some decades ago; the children were discussing their favorite movie stars.

Clark Gable, Tyrone Power, Betty Grable, Walter Pidgeon, Errol Flynn, Ginger Rogers, Greta Garbo, Roy Rogers—they were all getting into the act.

Finally, Amanda, a five-year-old, spoke up. "God's my favorite," she said.

"God's no movie actor," the others chimed in.

"Oh, yes, he is. He's the best."

"He is not," one of the boys said insistently. "He's no actor."

"He is so!"

"Where'd you get such a silly idea?" another child asked.

"Why it's right in the prayer: Our Father who art in heaven, Hollywood be thy name!"

TOWARD CLEARER VISION

The arrangement had been perfectly fair. Jimmy knew there was no justification for his being sad. Still, he could not hold back the tears.

The grandparents had thought three small fry, especially at the squirming, bickering ages of five to nine, were too many to take boating and picnicking at the same time, so had agreed to take one on Saturday and the other two the following week.

Jimmy had gone first, and he had had a glorious time. A fact, probably, that contributed to his gloom when, a few days later, he stood on the dock and waved goodbye as his older brother and sister sped off with Grandma and Grandpa.

"Why, Jimmy," his mother exclaimed, seeing his tears, "you shouldn't cry. You had your turn and you even got to go first."

"I'm not crying," he snapped, turning his head.

His mother put a sympathetic arm around him, and then turned his face to hers, and half comforting, half scolding, said, "Why, you are crying? Come on now, stop it."

"I am not crying," was the emphatic response. "My eyes are just taking a bath!"

TRAVEL BAG

The family was spending the day at the zoo, Mother, Dad, two older sons and four-year-old Jean.

Jean was delighted with the antics of the monkeys, enjoyed the fabulous colors of the exotic birds and finally stood in awe watching the elephant pacing back and forth in his huge cage.

When it came time to move on, the child asked, "Daddy, where's the elephant going?"

"Oh, he just walks back and forth in his cage. I guess he does that most all day."

"Yes, I see him walking in the cage, but where's he going?"

"Well, just back and forth."

The group turned to move on, all but Jean, who now raised her voice impatiently and half crying said, "I want to know where the elephant is going!" Father seemed a bit impatient too, "What do you mean 'going?'" he asked.

"I heard you say that he had a trunk!"

TRAVEL PROBLEMS

Dad had received a new atlas, and, as we all occasionally do, was taking an imaginary trip. Two-and-a-half-year-old Lisa crawled up on his lap and started asking questions.

First, Dad had to explain what a map was. Then he showed her the outline of the United States and then the outline of Minnesota. Then Dad turned to the state map and pinpointed Duluth where they lived.

"Where does Grandma live?" the child asked.

Dad flipped over to the Florida map and pointed out Fort Lauderdale. "Grandma lives right here," he explained. Then he turned back to the U.S.

map and put one finger on Duluth and another on Fort Lauderdale. "We live up here and Grandma lives down here in Florida."

The child seemed interested, but said nothing. The father only casually observed as the child got her doll, Polly, put on its dress, shoes, socks and bonnet. Then she opened the doll's suitcase and put in more doll clothes along with a tiny mirror, doll hair curlers and sundry items.

The child left the room and soon Dad heard the front door open. He arose and went to the front room. The child had put on her own coat and bonnet, now had Polly under her arm and was carrying the suitcase in the other hand as she walked down the sidewalk toward the curb. There she stopped and stood glancing around in all directions. This continued for perhaps five minutes.

Finally, the child broke into tears. She turned and walked back to the house. Now she was crying her heart out. Huge tears were running down her cheeks.

Dad went to the door. "Honey, what on earth's the matter?"

"Puh – puh – puh – Polly – wuh – wuh – wanted to g—g – go to Grandma's house, bu – but you won't let muh – muh – me cross the street."

TRIED SHADOWBOXING

The more children there are in a family, the more opportunity there is for sibling clashes. Freddy had quarreled with each of his three brothers and three sisters on this particular day.

"Freddy," his mother exclaimed, utterly exasperated, "what's the matter with you? Can't you get along with anybody?"

"It's not me, it's their fault," was the belligerent response, "I don't fight with anybody when I'm by myself!"

TWO PLACES AT ONCE

It was a fierce storm with lots of thunder and lightning. Three-year-old June was sitting tight up against her daddy on the sofa. "Daddy, will you sleep with me tonight?" she asked.

"No, you'll be all right, this storm will be over pretty soon."

"But, Daddy, I'm scared. I want you to sleep with me."

"No, I sleep with Mommy. God will be with you. He'll take good care of you."

"Well, where is he now?"

"He's right here. He's always here."

"He is not! On Sundays He's in church!"

UNBEARABLE STRESS

According to Carrie's mother, Robert Redford had nothing on Buster. Buster had it all, looks, personality, charisma, charm, allure, glamour, magnetism, you name it, and if any of those words are synonyms of each other, that still isn't overdoing it! Buster was a worldly three years old.

Competition among the three-year-old lassies in the preschool was fierce, but, wonder of wonders, Carrie emerged as the Chosen One.

"Can Buster come over and play?" "Can Buster stay for dinner?" "Can we buy Buster a tricycle too?" "Can I marry Buster when I grow up?" "How soon will that be?" "Can Buster stay overnight?" Then, after several pleadings on this last question, arrangements were made so that Buster could, indeed, stay overnight, there came (you probably foresaw it) the next logical question, "Can Buster sleep with me?"

The latter request was not granted, but it prompted Dad to say in a light vein to Mom, but in Carrie's presence, "I'm going to have to ask that Buster if his intentions are honorable."

Carrie didn't seem to notice the remark, but the next day after Dad had gone to work, Carrie asked, "Mommy, did Daddy ask Buster if his tensions are horrible?"

UNBELIEVABLE COINCIDENCE

Benjamin, five, and Joanna, seven, accompanied their parents when they were invited by friends to spend the weekend at the latter's lakeside cabin. The weather, as it turned out, was not conducive to outdoor activity, so most of the time was spent inside playing assorted games.

The adults were playing bridge and eventually Benjamin and Joanna got into a scrap about a deck of playing cards. The argument intensified and the children's mother demanded that they desist.

Benjamin began to cry and the hostess got up and said, "Benjamin, come with me." She rummaged around in the toy box and offered, "Here, would you like to play with these? Aren't they pretty pictures?"

"Yes, they're really pretty," the boy said. He took them to the bridge table and showed them to his mother. "Mommy, look at all these pretty pictures of blue jays."

"Oh, yes, they're nice," his mother said and then turned back to her game.

Benjamin laid all the pictures out on the floor. "One blue jay, two blue jays, three blue jays...," he counted.

Then he was quiet for a while as he shuffled the pictures around in different patterns. Suddenly he let out a shriek of delight. "Oh, look, look!" he exclaimed gleefully. "These pictures have cards on the backs of them!"

UNCARING MOTHER

Washing a child's mouth out with soap was the common reward for sassing in the Cranston home. It didn't occur often, but occasionally a disgruntled child allowed his frustrations to get the best of him.

In most homes, mild infractions are often overlooked. Probably this is no boon to discipline, but most parents succumb occasionally to some degree. And, so it was with Wendy and her mother. The first sassing brought no action, not even a reaction. Thus, the condition escalated.

Suddenly, Mother realized she was being sassed.

"Wendy, you come here," she commanded as she headed for the bathroom.

"I won't!"

"Young lady, you come, and you come now," her mother said, not raising her voice.

Overpowering the wriggling girl, she squeezed the child's mouth open and rubbed the bar of soap against her teeth, then forced it farther in her mouth.

Wendy began to cry and spit. "Remember that," her mother said, "next time you feel like you want to sass your mother." She walked calmly from the bathroom, closing the door.

But the child would not allow her mother the last word; she opened the door and said, "Well, you might at least have used Ivory Soap!"

UNFORBIDDEN FRUIT

After returning home from the supermarket, the Millers discovered their six-year-old son had a package of candy. Thinking back, they recalled, yes, this type of candy had been piled near the checkout counter; the child had simply slipped a sack into his pocket.

Immediately they lectured the child on taking property not his own, drove him back to the store where they sought out the manager, forcing the child to return the merchandise and apologize.

The Millers were highly pleased with the manager's skillful blending of firmness and kindness in reprimanding the child and came away feeling that the impression was profound and would be lasting.

It was two years later that the boy came home humming youthfully and munching an apple, his pockets bulging with more of the fruit.

"Where did you get those apples?" his father asked.

"Down there on Rosemont Avenue," the boy replied forthrightly. A bit more questioning pinpointed the precise location.

"That's stealing!" father Miller declared, astonished.

"No, it's not, it's okay with the owner."

But the parents couldn't accept this, they piled in the car and headed for Rosemont. As they turned onto the Avenue, sure enough…

Probably no adult on earth would place the same connotation on the two words, but to an eight-year-old, the message on the realtor's sign at the edge of the orchard made perfect sense:

"Will divide!"

UNINTENDED CONFESSION

One rule in the Montessori classroom is that a child does not interfere with another pupil's work.

Five-year-old Connie was doing some collage work with tissue paper in a shallow box and Jake, a three-year-old, was sitting nearby watching. Jake put his finger in the box and pushed down on the tissue paper.

"No, Jake," the teacher said, "you're not allowed to touch other people's work."

"Well," Jake replied, "I was just pushing it down so the paste would stick and the cover would fit on."

"But we must obey the rules," the teacher commented, "I know you only intended to help. You seem to have a logical, orderly mind."

Jake grinned at the compliment. "Gee, that's not what Mrs. Walker says."

"Oh? Who's Mrs. Walker?"

"She's the lady who helps my mother. She cleans my room."

UNIQUE APPENDAGE

Wendy's best friend, Terry, had a puppy which the two children often took for walks.

Eventually Wendy put on a campaign at home for a puppy of her very own. Finally her parents were persuaded. Since Terry's dog was small, Dad assumed Wendy wanted one similar. He checked some ads in the paper, and the family went scouting.

"No, that's not the kind I want," the child said as they checked out some poodles. Dad craftily avoided the more expensive breeds. They saw others but still the child said, "No, that's not the kind I want."

"Well, what do you want? Do you want a bigger dog?"

"No, I want a dog like Terry's."

So Dad scanned the ads for Scott Terriers and the family drove some thirty miles to see a brood of this breed.

"No, that isn't what I want."

"But, Wendy, this is the same kind Terry has, honestly it is."

"No, it isn't! No, it isn't! No, it isn't!"

A bit disgusted, Dad took Mom's arm and said, "Lets' go." Just then, a customer came in with a poodle on a leash.

"That's the kind I want! That's what I want!"

"But, Honey, that's a poodle. The first dogs we saw were poodles and you said that wasn't the kind you wanted."

"No, that isn't so. This one has a handle so I can take him for walks!"

UNIQUE BEDTIME STALL

When Stuart was four, his older brother experienced a shock when plugging in his electric train. He screamed and continued to cry for perhaps as long as ten minutes.

It came bedtime and Stuart was told to go upstairs and get ready for bed. He started to obey, but soon was back in the den with his books.

"Stuart," his mother said, "I told you to go get ready for bed."

"I know, but I can't."

"You can't? What do you mean, you can't?"

"It's dark upstairs."

"Well, turn on the light."

"I can't. My hands are scared!"

UNIQUE PASTIME

Grandpa and Grandma had Rachael for the week. The trio went fishing, and the child soon became bored as there was little action.

The grandparents fell to visiting about things that didn't interest Rachael, but after a while turned their attention to the child's direction to discover an amazing sight.

"Rachael, what on earth are you doing?" Grandma asked.

"Well, gee, there's nothing to do, I can't just sit here."

What they saw in the child's hands and extending down to the floor of the boat, was a wriggling mass of fish worms, tied tightly together in knots to form a two-foot-long string!

UNIQUE PERSUASION

Nine-year-old Peggy avoided water like the plague! Her parents and brother tried to get her to learn how to swim, or at least to go bathing in a lake or pool but she shunned the whole idea.

One delightful summer day she was enjoying the great outdoors, wandering more or less aimlessly in a field near a pond. She was clad only in a suit of bib overalls.

She was suddenly jerked into reality when she stepped in a nest of yellow jackets. The fact that her overalls fit loosely afforded the wasps easy access to the pants leg, up which they speedily ascended. That fact, also, that the garment was loose, enabled her to vacate it with one frantic shrug. Naked, shrieking, two great strides put her in the pond and, by what must have been pure instinct, she launched into a reasonable exact facsimile of the Australian crawl.

Today, thirteen-year-old Peggy avoids yellow jackets like the plague, but she swims like a fish!

UNIQUE REMEDY

In soliciting stories for this book, I talked to most anyone who would listen. Seeing a mother with one or more small children, I would explain my quest and give her a note with my name and phone number. Most always I would get a favorable promise, but, sorry to say, few delivered. More often, I might get a story right there on the spot.

On one occasion, I engaged an older man in conversation and told him the type of story I was seeking. We'll call him Mr. Collins. "Well, this one isn't funny," he said. "There's no punch line by the youngster, but I think you'll find it interesting and worthy of being included in your book." Indeed, I did. Here is his story:

> I was on my way to becoming a drunk, a bum. Of course, I would not admit this, even to myself. My wife had implored me to

join Alcoholics Anonymous, but of course I said I didn't need it…and, as a matter of fact, it turned out I didn't. My cure took a different turn, and that is the crux of my story.

My next door neighbor had been killed in an accident. He left a widow and three children, the youngest of which was Keith, a boy of six years. My wife and I had no children, and I took a shine to Keith and he sort of took one to me. I took him with me when I ran errands and took him fishing quite often, but as my interest in the bottle increased, I saw less of the lad. Maybe we'd do a little something once a week, but the relationship waned as my addiction deepened.

One wintry Saturday afternoon, I was walking over to the tavern just off Main Street. A six to eight-inch snow had fallen and I was wearing overshoes. I heard something and turned around to find Keith walking behind me. Trying to avoid getting the snow in the top of his overshoes, he was carefully stepping into the impressions I had made in the snow with my boots. "Mr. Collins" the boy said, "I'm following right in your footsteps."

Keith went on his way, and I went into the tavern. Usually I sat at the bar with 'the boys,' but Keith had sent me a powerful message, unknowingly to be sure, but nevertheless a powerful message, and I chose a small table in a rather obscure corner. I ordered a drink and paid for it. For all I know that drink is still sitting there. After about ten minutes I left the tavern without touching the booze. To this day, I have never taken another drink!

UNLICENSED BEAUTICIAN

Mama was washing the car when she heard crying coming from the house. She hurried in to find three-year-old Mary Ann in the bathroom crying her heart out. She was standing on a short stool before the lavatory.

The child's blonde curls were gone and Mother was aghast. The lavatory was filled with sudsy water and the child was slowly moving her hand around picking out clumps of hair.

"Mary Ann," her mother demanded, "what on earth have you done?"

Sobbing out of control, the child responded, "My – my – my curls were d—d—d—dirty, an –an—and, I – I – I wanted to – to – wa—wash them, an –an – and now I can – can – can't get them ba – back on!"

UNLIKELY COMBINATION

After dinner, Mom was explaining to her three-year-old son that there was going to be a new member of the family.

"Someday very soon, I'll be going to the hospital, and then in a few days I'll be bringing home a new baby. You're going to have a new little brother or sister."

"Why are you going to the hospital? Are you sick?"

"No, but both the little baby and I will need special care for a few days after the baby is born."

"Why?"

"Well, for the first few days, I'll have to rest, and the doctor will have to watch the baby to see that he's okay."

"Well, where's the baby now?"

"Haven't you noticed that I've been getting bigger around the waist, see?" she said, putting her hands on her abdomen and pulling her smock taut to show her shape.

The boy looked and seemed to be noticing the condition for the first time, but he seemed perplexed. "But where's the baby, where's the baby now?"

"Here, right here in my stomach."

"You mean right there with all that meat and potatoes?"

UNMISTAKEN IDENTITY

Dad had picked up Margaret Ann and Josh after the Saturday afternoon movie. Approaching a four-way stop, he came to a complete halt, then started forward. As he did so a car sped through the intersection without stopping, directly in front of him. It was before the days of seat belts, and when he slammed on the brakes, both children plunged forward onto the car floor.

Soon home, Dad comforted Josh who was shaken but not hurt, while Mom tended to a tiny cut on Margaret Ann's forehead.

"How on earth did it all happen?" her mother asked.

"Oh, this crazy guy, he was speeding right through the stop sign. He didn't even slow down, and Daddy had to stop real quick, and Josh and I went on the floor."

"And Daddy knew the guy that did it, too."

"Oh? How do you know that?"

"Because Daddy called to him by name."

"He did? Well who was it?"

"Oh, I don't remember. It was Summer Beach or something like that!"

UNSKILLED PREVARICATOR

Tara, at age five, sometimes strayed from the truth.

One evening at the dinner table, the child was dawdling over her food. "Tara," her mother asked, "were you snacking again this afternoon?"

"No."

"Tara?" her mother said sternly.

"No, I wasn't," the child insisted.

"Tara, no cookies? No candy? Nothing at all when you were over at Marsha's this afternoon?"

"No."

"Tara, you're lying."

"No, I am not."

"Yes, you are, Tara, you're telling a big lie."

"I am not. How do you know I'm lying?"

"Why, Tara, it's written all over your face. You're lying."

Tara looked surprised. She slipped off her chair and hurried down the hall.

Soon she came running back.

"Ha, ha, ha, *you're* the liar," she declared. "I went and looked in the mirror, and there is *nothing* written on my face!"

VALUABLE BY-PRODUCT

Dad had driven a sand point for a well at their summer cabin. It was necessary now to form a "pocket" around the point, this to be accomplished by continuous pumping to remove some of the nearby fine sand.

Dad decided that nine-year-old Jim and six-year-old Tom should not be exempt from the toil involved with a vacation home since their enjoyment was a paramount factor in the decision to own such property. Thus, the lads were set to the task of pumping.

It was no simple job. The boys pumped and they pumped. Jim created a little chant which he repeated between pants and in rhythm with his strokes; "Gotta get a pocket, gotta get a pocket, gotta get a pocket."

The pumping was yielding an exceedingly fine sand which accumulated on the ground as the water ran off down the slope.

On and on went the arduous task, Tom taking turns with his older brother. He had picked up the chant; then they began chanting it in unison, ever in rhythm with the endless strokes, "Gotta get a pocket, gotta get a pocket, gotta get a pocket!"

After a long stint, Jim, sweating and hot, paused for a moment's rest. "Well, one thing," he said, "whether Dad gets his pocket or not, at least we'll get a sand pile!"

VOICE FROM BEYOND

Mr. Hyland had ordered a headstone for his aunt who had died a year earlier. He took along his seven-year-old son, Richard, when he went with the cemetery custodian to designate the exact spot for the marker.

The custodian probed into the ground with a crowbar attempting to find the exact location of the vault. After many attempts the bar finally struck something solid and seeming metal. He jabbed three or four times, and the sound was consistent, indicating a firm object.

Richard stepped behind a tree and began singing a song which was popular at that time.

"I Hear You Knocking But You Can't Come In!"

WEENED

The object of the exercise was to teach the child to say, "My name is Beverly West and I live at 34 Oakwood Circle."

She was at a very tender age, but her parents were trying to teach her to thus identify herself in case she might ever become separated from them in a shopping mall, or by some accident or quirk of circumstances.

She was only beginning to pick up words and utter them understandably. She picked up a few from TV, in fact, frequently on the tube she heard someone say, "My name is So and So, and..." followed perhaps by an additional phrase, which sort of tied in with the phrase Mom and Dad were trying to teach her.

She finally got the name right: "My name is Beverly West." One could actually understand it. The coaching on TV was probably of some help. Then one day as her parents launched forth with a routine lesson, they led her, saying, "My name is... my name is..." whereupon the child picked right up on the lead, saying,

"My name is Beverly West and I'm an alcoholic!"

WELL, DID YOU TRY THE CAT?

It was back in the days when a minister's remuneration often came partly in the form of goods and services provided personally by members of the congregation.

Roberta had not yet learned the arts of diplomacy and finesse when her mother asked her to take part of a meatloaf next door to the pastor.

Roberta's presentation speech was as follows: "Here's some meatloaf Mama said to bring over to you. Dad had all he wanted, so did Sis. I don't like it, and the dog won't eat it either!"

WHAT YEAR?

Laura, four, and her friend Christina, seven, were playing, and Christina said she had learned how to tell time.

"That's nothing," Laura said. "Anybody can tell time."

"Oh, no, they can't. I'll bet you can't."

"Of course I can. It's easy."

"I'll bet you can't."

"I'll bet I can."

Christina went to the next room and brought back a clock. "Okay now, smarty, here's a clock. If you're so smart, tell me what time it is."

Laura took a casual glance at the clock and said, "It's Tuesday!"

WICKED STEPMOTHER

Charlene's parents were divorced. Fortunately, the relationship between her father and mother was not as rancorous as it is between many divorced couples.

Although Mother had custody, visitation worked out very amiably, and Mother encouraged the child to be with her father as often as feasible. Dad came and he went more or less as he chose.

Then suddenly there was a new development—Dad was going to remarry. The ceremony was in a distant city and after the newlyweds returned, Charlene was scheduled to spend Sunday with her father and his new wife.

Now, Charlene knew the tale of Cinderella well, and Snow White and the Seven Dwarfs was one of her favorite stories, so as her mother dressed her on Sunday morning, saying, "Now you be a good girl. I'm proud of you and your daddy's proud of you," the child cried: "Stepmother! Is she a stepmother?"

"Why, yes, of course. She's your new stepmother."

Charlene began to whimper, "Do you mean she's going to dress me in rags and make me scrub the floors?"

WILDLIFE ADVOCATE

In 1955 Tom was driving with his dad across Texas. "Dad," Tom asked unexpectedly, "would you mind stopping here and letting me get some turtles?"

His father pulled to a stop and Tom went up over a little hill and soon was back with two turtles.

"Are we in a big hurry, Dad?" Tom asked.

"Not particularly."

"Well would you mind if I got a few more?"

Dad moved the car a few hundred feet to a better parking spot. Tom took a carton from the car's trunk, and when he returned he had nine more turtles, each about seven inches long.

"That makes eleven, Tom, don't you want to get one more to make an even dozen?"

"No."

"Well, maybe you'd like to get one or two to take back to a friend."

There was no response from the boy who had now placed the carton on the car floor and was sitting in the front seat facing forward.

"Tom," Dad repeated, "wouldn't you like to get a turtle or two for friends?"

When there was still no reply, Dad looked at Tom and was surprised to see tears streaming down the boy's cheeks.

"Tom, what's the matter?" his dad asked.

And between sobs, the child replied, "Well, I'm not going to give any turtles to Stephen. He lets all his animals die!"

To check on some of the details of this story, I recently wrote Tom and received this letter which I believe is worth sharing:

> That turtle story remains etched in my mind even though it occurred 29 years ago. I always was somehow hooked on reptiles especially turtles. But, growing up in California prevented me from seeing any in the 'wild.' So, I read about them, their range, habitat, food, etc. On this long trip, I was determined to bring home a box turtle or two. Yet on the whole 4,000-mile trip, I saw none. As we passed out of the Oklahoma panhandle into Texas, I suddenly asked my dad to stop the car. I don't know why, but I was convinced that I would find a box turtle in this terrain off the road. I got out of the car and was back in less than 10 minutes with a turtle in each hand. I can't explain this apparent intuition, and, oddly enough, in the next 100 miles, we saw many along the road. I brought them back home to California. Four are still there at the same house, as far as I know. My mother moved from the house in 1984. The next owners 'adopted' the turtles.

WIZARD OF WALL STREET

The phone rang and nine-year-old Mike answered.

"Mike, let me talk to your mother."

"She can't come to the phone right now, Dad. She's in the shower."

"Well, okay, now, listen," said Mike's airline pilot father. "I have a very important message for you to give her. I want you to listen carefully and get it straight, and give it to her immediately when she's out of the shower."

"Okay, Dad."

"I've been trying to get Merrill Lynch on the phone, but the lines are all busy. We're leaving for Bangkok, and I've got to get back on the plane. Now you be sure to give your mother this message."

"Yes, Dad, I will. What's the message?"

Dad spelled out the message, then Mike went back and became absorbed in his TV program as he gobbled the remainder of his lunch.

Mom came out of the shower, but Mike totally forgot about the message from Dad.

Back at school, an hour or so later, he suddenly remembered.

In semi-panic, he walked up to the teacher. "Mrs. Bannister, I have to go use the phone. It's extremely important."

"So important it can't wait till after school?'

"Oh, yes, I've got to call right now."

"Well, you can go on down to the principal's office and ask to use his phone, and he can decide."

Mike ran, he didn't walk, to the principal's office. "Mr. Price, I've got to use the phone right away. It's very important."

"You're welcome to use the phone, but can't you call after school? Your studies are important, too, you know."

"Yes, I know, but this is very, very, very important."

"Very well, if it's really that important you may use the phone here on my desk, but make it just as short as you can."

Now, dear reader, you must get this picture: Here stands a nine-year-old boy, with an extremely serious, worried expression on his face. Here sits the principal of the school, his hands folded, scrutinizing the lad closely, his countenance severe. In a corner of the room, a secretary stops her typing, turns her head to look at the boy. The lad dials the phone.

"Hello, Mom! Mom, this is extremely important! Call Merrill Lynch right away and order five hundred shares of Northwest Airlines!"

WOMEN MAKE BETTER PURCHASING AGENTS

The family lived on a farm on the outskirts of a Boston suburb. This was back in the days when many items of merchandise were simply unavailable in outlying communities, and transportation into the city was not as simple as it is today. Thus, an excursion into Boston was something of an event. When such a trip was planned, the children often had special requests for items they hoped their parent(s) would buy for them.

One day, Father was going into Boston on some errands, and Mary, age four and the youngest of three children, asked, "Daddy, could you buy us a new baby in Boston?" Another thing about "those days," the subject of human reproduction was not bantered about lightly, especially in the presence of the children.

Her father chuckled, "Sorry, Honey, it's a little more complicated than that. You can't just go into Boston and buy a baby." But there was a twinkle in his eye as he spoke. He knew what none of the children knew. A very special event was scheduled to occur in approximately four months.

Dad went into Boston about once a month and each time Mary would repeat her request for him to buy a baby, and each time he would side-step the issue with a smile, a chuckle or a few words of chitchat.

Finally came the day when there was a sudden bustle around the house. Nathan, the oldest son, was told by Mama to call Daddy in from the field where he was mending a fence. A suitcase was hastily packed. Aunt Georgia was called to come in and stay with the children, and Dad took off for Boston. This time he took Mama. As they went out the door, Mary once again repeated her request which had now become routine.

In a few hours, the news broke. Aunt Georgia announced to the children that Mom and Dad would be bringing home a new baby brother.

When the parents returned home, much ado was made over the event, and Mary said to her mother, "Gee, Mommy, you're smart. Daddy went into Boston every month and he couldn't buy a baby, and you only had to go once and you got a baby right away!"

YOU GO TO THE ALTAR, YOU TAKE YOUR CHANCES

Dawn, at the age of five, was very fond of her grandfather. She looked forward to her visit at Grandfather's acreage in June, and, on the first day, followed him around like a little puppy dog, jabbering at him constantly. Grandfather obviously liked the program and responded by laughing and returning the chitchat.

It was Grandfather's habit to retire early and Dawn climbed in bed with him, chattering, tickling, giggling and doing whatever might so amuse Grandfather that she could postpone the time when she'd have to go to her own bed.

Finally Grandmother came to the door and suggested that Grandfather was probably tired and would like to get to sleep. Grandfather failed to second the motion and Dawn was silent for only a few seconds and then was right back at the game.

After perhaps ten minutes, Grandmother again came to the door. "Dawn," she said, "your granddad works hard at the chores around this place and he needs his sleep. You come on now and get in your own bed."

Everything was quiet again for a few seconds, the only sound being that of Grandma's footsteps as she retreated once again down the hall. Then there was an unrestrained burst of giggling. This brought Grandma right back to the bedroom with a heavy and hastened step.

"Dawn," she commanded, "you come here this instant. I'm putting you in your own bed!"

"Okay, Grandma, I'll be right there, but I have just one question I want to ask Grandpa first."

"Oh well, all right, but you be quick about it!" And she again padded off down the hall.

Dawn turned to Grandpa and lowered her voice, "Grandpa, when you married Grandma did you know she was going to turn out like that?"

YOUNG PHILOSOPHER LOOKS AT THE FUTURE

Nine-year-old Jason was in a serious mood. "Ya know, Mom," he said, "when I grow up I don't think I'm going to be able to get married."

"Oh, but why not?" his surprised mother asked.

"Well, I wouldn't want to marry anyone who smoked or drank alcohol."

"Oh, but Honey, that's a long way off for you. By the time you're old enough to marry, you'll know lots of different girls, and surely some that don't smoke or drink."

"Yeah, but, Mom, another thing. I wouldn't want her to work, 'cause then she wouldn't be home and our kids would have to go to a daycare center, and those people there don't love kids like their parents do, and when kids don't grow up with people that love them, they get in all kinds of trouble and even sometimes have to go to jail!"

YOU'RE WRONG THERE, MOM!

Chuck was eight years older than Mary Ann and thus had the edge on her in many ways: bedtime, freedom, worldliness, etc.

This, coupled with the fact that Mary Ann had grown to age nine hearing their mother constantly scold Chuck about his disorderliness, just might be the reason that she, Mary Ann, was tidy and neat. Maybe she purposely excelled here, having sensed that this was one area in which she could outshine her older brother.

When Chuck was seventeen, a friend wanted him to go to Des Moines, thirty miles distant, to keep him company. Chuck's mother was agreeable but didn't want him to go without any funds.

"Now look, Chuck," she said, "you take this fifteen dollars just so you'll have some money in case of an emergency of some kind. You are not to spend it. Oh well, you could have a coke or something, but you are absolutely not to spend it for anything else unless an emergency should come up. Now is that understood?"

"Yeah Mom, sure Mom."

But when the lad returned he was carrying a package under his arm.

His mother eyed the package suspiciously. "Chuck," she said, "give me my fifteen dollars."

"I don't have it, I bought these jungle pants," he said as he removed a pair of trousers from the package. "Aren't they jazzy, Mom?"

This incident occurred back in the days when money was tight, and his mother exploded.

"I told you," she stormed, "that that money was to be used for emergency only!" She was obviously enraged.

Chuck only grinned and said, "Well, you told me I could get a coke or something and these pants are something!"

"You've got plenty of clothes, she went on, you need a pair of jungle pants like you need a hole in your head! Lord knows you seem to have plenty of those, and besides there isn't a *jungle* within a million miles of here!"

It was then that nine-year-old Mary Ann chimed in, "Oh, no? Have you seen his room lately, Mom?"

2. THE AUTHOR REMEMBERS HIS OWN CHILDHOOD

FLY IN THE OINTMENT

Jean, my next door neighbor, was about twelve, and I was three years her junior. I was sweet on her in a manner befitting our ages. My friend, John, also liked her, but there was no sense of competition between us, and, in fact, we more or less shared any pleasure when either of us was successful in gaining her attention.

For some time, we had been throwing kisses to her without any success in getting her to reciprocate. Finally I scored. From my back yard I threw a kiss through her kitchen window and she threw one back. This was a great milestone! I immediately got John on the phone and reported the achievement. Then I ran out in the yard again to throw kisses across the driveway. Each kiss was returned—one for one—kiss for kiss. Wow! What a triumph! This continued for several days. I never missed a ticket.

The first time John was over, I offered a demonstration. It was late afternoon, the usual time for the preparation of dinner, and, sure enough, Jean was in the kitchen. John observed. My right hand started gyrating, from my mouth toward the kitchen window, again and again and again, but the response was not as I had advertised. Jean doubled up with laughter. Her mother's face soon appeared at the window, and she, too, burst into laughter.

I was at a loss to understand this devastating humiliation. I turned to go in the house, my tail between my legs, John right behind me.

At the porch door my mother met me. "Robert," she screamed as a shocked expression swept over her face, "your pants, the fly on your pants is wide open!"

NINE CENTS A LOAF

John was my best friend and he lived next door. Every school morning, he would stop by and whistle for me and we would walk to school together.

We always came home for lunch and one noon his mother called to him, "John, I want you to go to the store and get a loaf of bread, here's a dime. You can have the change."

"Bob," John said, "come on, go with me."

"I can't," I said, "my mom's expecting me home."

"Oh, come on, I'll buy you a sucker."

"Butterscotch?" I asked.

"Sure, butterscotch, any kind you like."

"Okay, if we hurry," I said.

John got the bread and handed Mr. Moehler the dime and Mr. Moehler gave John a penny.

"Don't I get two pennies?" John asked.

"No, John, bread is nine cents now."

We went into the drug store. John set the grocery sack on the counter and asked the druggist, "Mr. Hanson, how much are butterscotch suckers?"

"A penny each, John."

"Okay, I'll take one butterscotch sucker."

John gave the penny to Mr. Hanson, took the sucker, removed its wrapping and plunked the sucker in his mouth.

"You promised me the sucker," I said when we were outside.

John muttered something, but I couldn't understand it because his mouth was full of sucker.

"John," I said again, "you promised me the sucker if I'd come to the store with you."

He took the sucker out of his mouth just long enough to say, "Wait, I'll give it to you." Then he plunked it again into his mouth.

About halfway home he took the sucker out of his mouth and handed it to me. "Here," he said. I didn't much care for the idea, but I did like butterscotch, so I put the sucker in my mouth.

When we got to John's house, his mother was on the porch, "John," she said, "where's the bread?"

A real funny look came over John's face. "I – I – I forgot and left it on the counter down at Hanson Drug."

His mother got really mad. "You get yourself right back down to Hanson Drug, and you get that bread and you be darn quick about it!"

"Come on, Bob. Go with me," John said.

I took the sucker out of my mouth and said, "I can't. I'm late home already."

"You come with me, or you can't have the sucker!"

"You promised me the sucker and you gave it to me." I replied.

John reached over and grabbed the sucker out of my hand, put it in his mouth and started walking away fast.

"I hate you," I shouted.

"Who cares? I never did like you anyway."

He went his way and I went mine. When I came home from school after the afternoon session, I went around by Harwood Drive, so I would be sure not to run into John.

That night I cried because I had lost my best friend and I knew I would never have another.

The next morning, I was dawdling over breakfast and my mother said, "You'd better hurry or you'll be late for school. John will be here any minute."

"John's not coming," I said. I didn't have to explain to my mother, because just as I spoke, I heard John's whistle.

Throughout all of our growing up together, the events of that terrible day of the butterscotch sucker were never mentioned again.

TESTING

My mother was a member of the Sunset Study club. The group met periodically, one member reporting on some field of knowledge on which she had made a special study.

On this particular day, the meeting was at our house. When I came home from school the group of approximately twelve ladies was seated around our living room. The stairway was immediately adjacent to this room.

I do not recall what brought my mother and me to the foot of the stairs or what was the subject of our conversation, but I do know we were having a controversy about something, probably some chore that I should attend to, perhaps home work, and I was being contrary.

I do recall that I finally said to her in a loud, clear voice, "I'll spit in your face." And I recall as vividly as though it had happened just yesterday, one additional detail: my eyes went slowly but definitely to the face of each and every woman that I could see from where I stood. I was looking for reaction. I remember only a silence—silence as though the whole world had stopped dead still.

My mother said nothing further. I remember nothing further.

The matter was never mentioned again.

WARNING SIGNAL

I was delighted when our family got a beautiful little orange and white kitten. She was very playful and brought me a lot of pleasure.

I had never heard a cat purr nor had I even heard this phenomenon mentioned.

One day I was lying with my head on the cat. Suddenly I went running to my mother, crying, "Mommy, mommy, our kitty is going to die!"

"Oh, no Honey," she responded, "what makes you think so?"

"Oh, I can hear all the little germs working inside her!"

3. A FEW STORIES OF THE AUTHOR'S KIDS

ACCIDENTAL INDEED!

The matter of health and accident insurance came up in the presence of our son, Bob Jr. I do not recall the nature of the basic discussion, but he wanted to know the difference between "health" and "accident."

"Health is involved with sickness, and to be injured in an automobile wreck would be an accident," I explained.

He seemed confused. "But I still don't see any difference," he replied.

"Well, just take my own case," I said, trying to be more explicit. "Remember last Christmas when I fell on the stairs and broke a bone in my foot? That was an accident. But when I got the mumps this spring, that was a sickness, a matter of health."

However, his face did not brighten; his expression looked even more puzzled. "But I just don't understand it. When somebody gets sick, wouldn't that be an accident, too? You surely didn't get the mumps on purpose!"

ACHES AND PAINS

PART I

Charlotte and I took an early morning hike in Yosemite National Park. It turned out to be too long a walk for her young muscles and finally she slowed her pace, complaining, "Gee, (puff, puff) Dad, (puff, puff) my feet are (puff, puff) getting a headache!"

PART II

Returning home after a vacation, we found eighteen small window glasses broken out by vandals.

Although the insurance settlement had been adequate, I was determined to earn a little extra cash by doing the labor myself.

I'm mostly all thumbs when it comes to this kind of job so my mood was not the best along toward the end of that Saturday and this was obvious to Charlotte.

Finally, I was down to the cleaning operation, scraping with a razor blade vigorously, and was talking mainly to myself when I said, "Gee, makes me mad that they've got to put a sticker on each and every one of these new windows!"

"Hey, Dad," Charlotte asked in an attempt to raise my spirits, "do you suppose that's why they are called panes?"

CRISIS AT THE MAGIC HOUR

Yes, the kids, especially three-year-old Bobby, had asked me to get the Christmas tree lights to replace those that were "out." But with the press of holiday chores coupled with my failure to put the item on a written list, the evening of December twenty-fourth arrived and still I had not made the necessary purchase.

Therefore, at five p.m., I was clearly in the dog house, and knew I must obtain the bulbs at all costs.

After a quick supper, I ventured forth at the late hour to do the necessary, but alas, other people were bent on enjoying their holiday too, and I found store after store closed and finally returned home empty handed.

Disappointment was obvious, but no one really denounced me.

At ten o'clock it was up the stairs to bed. I tucked Bobby in, turned out the light and was closing the door when he struck his final blow:

"Boy, that Santa Claus is really going to be mad when he sees that Christmas tree!"

MARILYN FLUNKS BIOLOGY

Had Princie been a smaller dog, it might have made more sense, but he was a collie and weighed perhaps forty pounds.

The children were with their mother at our summer place in Northern Minnesota.

Marilyn, then nine, came running to her mother, "Mommy," she declared, "Princie has two wood ticks on him. Oh, they're huge! Oh, they're just awful! Oh, Mommy, what are we going to do?"

Having no particular desire to view the ugly sight, the children's mother simply piled Princie, Marilyn and the two younger children in the car and drove the thirty miles to town.

"Princie has some wood ticks the doctor's going to have to remove," Mom said to the receptionist.

"Okay, he'll be right with you."

The veterinarian put the dog on his table and asked Marilyn to step up and show him where the ticks were.

Now as I progressed with this book, stories came to me which required that I make a decision. Would I or would I not include an X-rated chapter? I decided that I would not.

This story tended toward the X-rated, yet seemed too good to omit, so in view of these factors, I had best conclude this story by saying that when Marilyn pointed out the "ticks" to the vet, he simply doubled up in laughter!

NO SYSTEM IS PERFECT

In our household, as doubtless in many, we had a condition known as "on silence." When things among the children got so boisterous as to be on the verge of getting out of hand, one or more of them was put "on silence," which meant the obvious.

It was at the dinner table one evening that it happened to Bobby. He had been especially effervescent, so I leveled an index finger at him and with a stern look declared, "You're on silence!" After a few minutes, he came on with the test routine, mumbling something to see if I'd forgotten, and I descended on him in a manner that convinced him I hadn't!

About five minutes later, he raised his hand.

"No, you're on silence!" I barked.

Now it was not in the rules that he could not raise his hand, and he kept it raised. Soon he was lowering and raising it, full height, with a jerking motion. We saw him, his mother and I, but pretended not to notice. Our two daughters, now that one of the threesome was quelled, were behaving well.

Now Bobby was jerking his hand and arm as though to pull them from their sockets. Still I did not acquiesce. This continued for several minutes.

And then from afar off, I heard an ominous sound. It came closer, then much closer, and even then I did not connect this sound with our dinner table events. But when the screeching fire engine came to a halt in front of our house and I jumped to the window, it became obvious to me that all along Bobby had had a direct view of our neighbor's flaming roof!

PLEA OF NOT GUILTY

When Bobby was four, his mother's sister came to visit, and brought as a gift a very unusual and attractive candy dish. Only minutes after it had been unwrapped, the ladies went to the kitchen to prepare a snack. They were engaged in sister talk when suddenly there came from the family room a violent crash. They froze, knowing full well what had happened. There was utter silence for several seconds, then a heart rending cry.

They found Bobby standing over the major portions of the broken dish. Its splinters scattered over a radius of several feet. He looked up at them, then down at the fragments, crying uncontrollably. It was a minute or two before he could verbalize. Then, still crying, he shook his head negatively, "I didn't break it! I didn't break it!" he insisted.

But there was no one else in the room; he was poised directly over the ruins; his guilt was indisputable. Although she felt compassion, his mother also felt constrained to force the truth from him.

"You didn't break it? Well, then who did? You were the only one here."

Still sobbing, "Yes, but I didn't break it. I only dropped it. The floor broke it!"

POLLUTION

You've probably known the type. The kid that doesn't want his food contaminated—like, for instance the peas touching the mashed potatoes, and if the squash touches the meat, they're both "spoiled."

Bobby, at age nine, was one of those, and what drove him absolutely bonkers was when his mother took his year-old sister's undrunk milk and poured it back in the bottle. The thought of seeing Charlotte's baby food smeared around her mouth, the milk glass touched to it, and then the remaining milk returned to the container from which he might be served, devastated him. As a result, he developed the habit of pouring his own milk and always from either a theretofore unopened bottle or one that had been constantly under his surveillance since being opened. The dairy delivered to our home quart bottles of the product three times a week, and often we would have as many as five bottles on hand.

Like many children, Bobby was frequently late for meals as he was prone to linger with his playmates or at some activity that absorbed him. His mother and older sister decided to teach him two lessons in one whammy: be on time for meals, and don't be so everlastingly picky about your "dirty" food.

Bobby is now forty-five and he still tells this story of how he was shaken to the core!

As our meal started—no Bobby—and the plot was set. Half way through the meal he came bouncing in, his normal effervescent self. He went jauntily to the refrigerator, opened the door, and there was confronted with five bottles of milk, lined in their usual place each of which was but three-quarters full!

SIBLING ALLIANCE

Siblings will scrap and battle to within an inch of their lives, then at other times, come scrambling to the defense or aid of each other. It was thus with our three.

Marilyn, at age sixteen, was being punished for lying, and was grounded for a month. Being "grounded" meant that she had to come directly home from school and could not go out in the evenings. She had been caught cold, and once she knew it, she recognized that there was no out. She took it in good spirit, did not pout nor complain.

Before the month was up, she was invited to a party. I told her no, the grounding was for a month, and a month it would be. She was deeply disappointed, and it became obvious that she set out to form a sibling alliance, for the next day, son Bob Jr., age fourteen, approached me.

"Dad," he said, "hasn't Marilyn been real good since you grounded her?"

"Yes, she has."

"Well then, why don't you let her go to Reece's party? It's not like she's just going to go out and run around. There'll be adults there and everything."

"But, Bob," I said, "what is punishment? The very essence of punishment is that the person punished be deprived of that which he would want to do. Otherwise, how could you call it punishment?"

The next day it was Charlotte, at the tender age of four. Her plea was simple and to the point. "Daddy, won't you please let Marilyn go to Reece's party?"

"No, Charlotte, I just can't do that. What good is punishment if the person being punished can do those same things that he could have done if he were not being punished?"

But Charlotte didn't give up with this. Sisters have to stick together. "But, Daddy, you've got to 'sidder this: Marilyn isn't really bad. Next to me, she's the best daughter you have!"

THEN CAME MONDAY

Routinely, when Bobby would say, "I'm thirsty," I would respond jokingly with, "I'm Friday."

This went on for a long time until finally one day he not only topped me but forced me to follow through and provide the treats!

"I'm thirsty," he said one hot summer day.

"I'm Friday," I responded.

"I'm Saturday. Will you buy me a sundae?"

UPSET STOMACH

The first long trip we made in Pinky—our new car, so named because of its bright coral color—took us to the west coast.

We had been on a slow, steady climb for many miles when we saw a sign, "Spring Water." The day was delightful, the scenery gorgeous, the forest verdure invigorating, and the thought of a drink of cool, mountain water appealed to all of us.

We parked and piled out of the car. Since we had been climbing for some time, it occurred to me the car might need a drink also, but my mind was not in gear when I removed the radiator cap. Steam and boiling water belched forth, shooting, geyser-like, high into the air. I lurched back, but not quickly enough to escape the scalding stream which caught the under side of my arm from wrist to elbow, and I cried out in pain!

My wife and two older children, in their early teens, rushed to my aid while three-year-old Charlotte froze with fright as steam and liquid continued to hiss and bubble from the car.

Minutes passed. My arm grew red and stung like crazy. We had no first aid supplies. We lingered. Very quickly I felt better. It became obvious my burn was not serious. Our mood normalized.

We allowed the car to cool, filled the radiator with water, had another drink, and were on our way.

All this time Charlotte had not spoken—not in the short moment of panic when the rest of us chattered excitedly, nor afterwards when the talk was again relaxed and cheerful.

It was perhaps a half-hour later, there had come a lull in our conversation. Charlotte broke it with three words from the back seat: "Pinky threw up!"

INNOCENCE AND SPICE

Often it is the complete innocence of a child's utterance that gives it charm and amusement, as in the incident just related. However, the spice Charlotte added to our fishing trip one day arose from a willful flaunting of her sense of humor.

Because we would be in a canoe, I provided coffee cans of worms for each of us, so we would not be tipping the craft by passing the bait back and forth.

Purposely I took Char to a spot where there would be lots of action, though the fish were small. She was seven.

I caught fish, one after the other, throwing most of them back. She got bites constantly, but landed practically nothing, and she grew impatient.

"Daddy, why do you catch them and I can't? Is there something wrong with my pole?"

"No, there's nothing wrong with your pole."

A minute later: "Daddy, is there something wrong with my line?"

"No, there's nothing wrong with your line."

"Is there something wrong with my hook?"

"Well, let me look at it," she hoisted it up to me, and I inspected it. "No, there's nothing wrong with your hook."

Another minute: "Is there something wrong with my sinker?"

I'm sure a faint hint of exasperation was creeping into my voice by this time. "No," I was emphatic, "there's nothing wrong with your sinker!"

"Is there something wrong with my worms?"

No doubt about it, she could surely discern disgust in my voice now. "No, for gosh sakes, our worms are the same!"

"Oh, no, they're not," she declared triumphantly.

"Yours are Folgers and mine are Maxwell House!"

4. A KID OF THE AUTHOR REMEMBERS MORE STORIES

I know that my father would not have objected to me adding a few more stories because he was constantly bugging me for them since I worked with children every day. So here are a few more written by me.

Charlotte

ADOPTION OPTION

Dan, my husband, and I adopted our two girls; they are from the country of South Korea. Dan and I are Caucasian.

When Samantha was in early elementary school, her friend Alec was shocked to hear she was adopted.

"No! You are *not* adopted!" he asserted.

"Yes, I am!" she stated with gusto.

"There is no way you are adopted!"

"Yes, I am! I'm from South Korea!"

"But you look *exactly* like your parents!"

"No, I don't. I have dark brown hair and brown eyes. My nose is small and flat, and my eyes slant."

Pause.

"Oh."

Longer pause.

"I guess you don't look like your parents. I guess you are adopted."

BABIES COME FROM AIRPORTS

Cassie, our oldest daughter, always knew she was adopted. She had seen the pictures and watched the videos of the day we picked her up at the airport.

When she was about five years old, we had some friends over for dinner and they had a daughter, Kaitlyn, about a year older than Cassie. The two of them hit it off immediately and trotted off to Cassie's room to play. At the end of the visit, the parents announced to the children that it was time to go.

As Cassie was walking Kaitlyn to the door to say good bye, we heard Cassie say, "My parents got me at the Minneapolis airport. What airport did your parents get you at?"

FLOWER REPAIRMAN

My nephew, Charly, was very, very orderly at age two, as is common for children of that age. Everything had a place, and everything was to be in its place.

His father found him in the front yard attempting to pick up the petals that had fallen from the flowers, and trying to put them back on the flower. They would of course, fall off again, and he would patiently bend down and pick them up and try to replace them.

After he had done this for about 20 minutes, his father asked him what he was doing, and he said, "Trying to fix the flowers."

FUTURE NEGOTIATOR

Two children were running around the classroom, so I sent them to time-out. I walked by one of them sitting in a chair.

Child: "We were just playing ghost busters."

Me: "Well, you shouldn't be playing ghost busters in school when you are supposed to be working."

Child: "Couldn't you just change that rule?"

I'D DRIVE A MILE FOR A WONTON

When our two daughters were little, we sometimes went to South Carolina to visit my sister and her husband for Christmas. We always drove, and from Minnesota it took us two days.

One year a snow storm was predicted at the same time we were planning our return home, so we decided to leave a day early. We quickly packed our bags, then went to a Chinese restaurant for dinner. We told the children that we would be leaving early the next morning; that we would be driving straight through and not making any stops other than to get gas, go to the bathroom and pick up food because we wanted to miss the storm.

The next day we drove, drove, drove all morning; drove, drove, drove all day; and drove, drove, drove into the early evening. At 8:00 p.m. we were far enough ahead of the storm to be safe, so figured we could finally take a rest and stop for dinner. So we asked the girls where they would like to eat.

Samantha, age four, replied, "Could we eat at that Chinese restaurant where we ate last night?"

LAPTOP SOLUTION

When I was a child our family lived in Des Moines, Iowa. Every year, the day after the last day of school, we would get in the car, drive for about ten to twelve hours to arrive at our cabin on Lake Vermilion in northern Minnesota. My dad would open up the cabin, put the dock in the water, get the boat ready for use, and get us all set up for lake life for the summer. He stayed for a week and then went back to Des Moines while my mother, my two siblings and I stayed at the lake.

In July Dad would return and he would take us on lots of lake adventures: to see Indian graves, to travel to a small town by boat, to go to a remote sandy beach to swim, and so on. It was a lot of fun. Then at the end of the week, he drove back home.

At the end of August, one week before the start of school, Dad would come back. He took out the dock, winterized the boat and closed down the cabin; and the day before school started, we would pile in the car and make the long trip back to Des Moines.

I loved the lake and cherish my childhood memories there, but it is too bad my dad couldn't have spent more time with us during all those summers.

I had relayed this story and my sentiments to our children when ten-year-old Cassie asked, "Well, why didn't he stay all summer?"

"Because he had to work," I answered.

Then came the next obvious question, "Why didn't he just bring his laptop instead?"

LOOPHOLE THINKER

Boyd, age five, was an excellent student, and normally well-behaved, but he had his moments when he could be defiant and quite stubborn. He needed to do some additional practice in building words so I told him to take out the movable alphabet. He walked away from me.

"Boyd. Take it out."

He ignored me.

"Boyd, I said to take it out."

No response.

"Boyd!"

"I'll take it out, but I won't do it."

"And do it," I added.

"I won't do it right."

"And do it right."

NOT SO FAMOUS AUTHOR

When my book, *Montessori: Why It Matters for your Child's Success and Happiness,* was released, I showed it to all the children in my classroom. They were delighted to see pictures of each other inside the book, as well as Morgan, my granddaughter, on the cover. The book was displayed in the main hallway into the school and Morgan walked by it every day to and from class.

One day a year later, several children ages five and six were laying on the floor writing stories. Hazel finished her first sentence and said, "This is the hardest thing I have ever done in my entire life!"

"Oh, Hazel," I joked, "you'll probably grow up and write lots of stuff and become a famous author just like me."

Morgan glared at me as if she had just caught me in a lie. "You're not an author. You're just a teacher."

"I am a teacher, but I am also an author," I said.

"Oh really? What have you written?"

NOT SO YUCKY AFTER ALL

It was lunchtime at school and the children were trying to decide where to sit so they could eat.

I walked in between the tables teasing the girls, "Ew, you wouldn't want to sit there. There's a boy!" "Ew, yuck, there's another boy!" "Not there! One of those boys!" "Boys, boys everywhere! Ick!"

I continued in this manner, giggling and taunting until Jack, age 5, stopped me dead in my tracks. "Why, Miss Char! How can you say that about us boys when we have all those *manly* powers!"

PAINFUL LESSON

Samantha, age five, had hurt herself and I put some medication on her small wound.

Samantha then asked, "Will the pain go away?"

I answered, "No, you're going to hurt for a while."

Samantha then immediately went downstairs to her sister's room and made an important announcement. Then for the next several days she was in constant trouble for hitting, poking, scratching and punching her sister.

The time-outs and consequences for her misbehavior were getting nowhere so in desperation, I got right in Samantha's face, nose to nose, and gave her the riot act. "But Mommy," Samantha said, "you told me I was going to hurt for a while, remember?"

PAY ATTENTION, GRANDPA!

A small girl, aged four or five, was visiting with her grandpa. He asked her a question, and she answered it, but Grandpa wasn't quite sure what she meant, so he asked the question in a slightly different way. The little girl looked at him and answered, "You don't listen very well for someone your age."

PLASTIC SNACK

In my Montessori classroom, the children managed their own snacks independently. Upon arrival to school the children would put their snacks in their snack drawers. Then during work time if they wanted to eat and there was room at the snack table, they would go to their drawer, get their snack, sit down and eat it. This worked well overall, but occasionally a child would eat someone else's food by accident.

One day someone had eaten Tom's cheese and crackers, so I rang the bell, waited for the children to stop and listen, and asked if anyone knew what had happened to Tom's snack. No one said anything. So we looked in the garbage. A-ha! There were the plastic wrappings.

I held them up and said, "Who had this for snack?"

Brittany, an absolutely adorable two-year-old, raised her hand.

At the end of class time, when Brittany's mother came to pick her up, Brittany walked directly over to her and proudly announced that she had eaten plastic at school.

TUMMY LOVE

The George family had three children: Missy, Charly and Kelly. Charly had been adopted shortly after his birth which Charly knew because his parents had always been honest about this fact.

Charly didn't seem too curious to know more about his arrival into the family until he was four years old when one day he asked his mother, "Why didn't I come out of your tummy?" She responded that it was because he was adopted, and that he had come out of another woman's tummy.

The next day he asked the same question whereupon his mother explained it again, this time adding some more details about the adoption process, hoping that this would satisfy him.

But it did not. Day after day, week after week, Charly kept asking the same question, and day after day and week after week his mother explained it to him in as many different ways as she could think of in order to help him understand.

Then one night at dinner Charly asked, what was by now, his predictable question, "Why didn't I come out of Mommy's tummy?"

His father immediately answered, "I didn't come out of Mommy's tummy either and she loves me."

Charly never asked that question again.

UNEXPECTED MARATHON

Bob, my brother, and his wife, Romie, had two children, both boys, ages six and four. I liked to visit them, it was always fun and this particular evening was especially amusing.

The bedtime routine was finished and the children were comfortably in bed. The three of us decided to go downstairs to the family room to watch television. An hour later, we were engrossed in a plot of a movie and all was quiet except for the goings on in the story.

All of a sudden my brother breaks the mood of deep concentration. He loudly calls out, "I'm going to go upstairs and if I find anybody out of bed, they're going to get a black and blue bottom from me!"

Immediately the sound of running feet could be heard up above headed towards the bedrooms as we roared with laughter.

WORLD TRAVELERS

Several four and five-year-old children were sitting around a table in the language area of my classroom, doing their work and conversing as they did so.

First child: "I've been to Mexico."

Second child: "I've been to Texas."

Third child: "I've been to McDonald's."

ABOUT THE AUTHOR

Bob Cushman was born in Des Moines, Iowa on February 20, 1912, where he was raised. He graduated from Roosevelt High School. After graduating from Grinnell College, he returned to Des Moines and became vice-president of Cushman-Wilson Oil Company, an oil distributor in Iowa. He was active in the Iowa Independent Oil Jobbers Association, chairman of the Des Moines Convention Bureau, chairman for three years for the Good Will Tours, active in Kiwanis, director of the Greater Des Moines Chamber of Commerce, a member of the Terpsichorean Dance

Club, a member of the Ad Club, active in the Jobbers Terminal Warehouse in Minneapolis, and one of the founders of the Bear Club where he held high prestigious honors. He retired in 1969 and spent his retirement years at his cabin on Lake Vermilion, Minnesota, as well as traveling to Mexico and the Southwest. He died on May 12, 1994 in Duluth, Minnesota.

He was a busy guy, but he always liked to write and would plunk away at his typewriter in the basement at his home. He had several articles published in various periodicals such as "Motor Home Life" and "Parents Magazine." He also wrote an autobiography, summaries of his travels, short stories and poetry.

Besides writing he also enjoyed boating, creating his own merriment (such as the Bear Club) and spending time with loved ones. He also took great pleasure in intellectual discussions and taught his children how to think by asking questions which pointed out the contradictions in an inaccurate viewpoint. He would also tell riddles to his children, but then did not tell them the answers—they had to figure them out for themselves.

Bob Cushman was raised the old fashioned way and grew up with morals, integrity and a delightful sense of humor. He was a genteel, fun-loving man who is remembered for his honesty, friendliness, logical mind and love of his country and the free enterprise system. His children adored him.

www.ingramcontent.com/pod-product-compliance
Lightning Source LLC
Chambersburg PA
CBHW051749040426
42446CB00007B/283